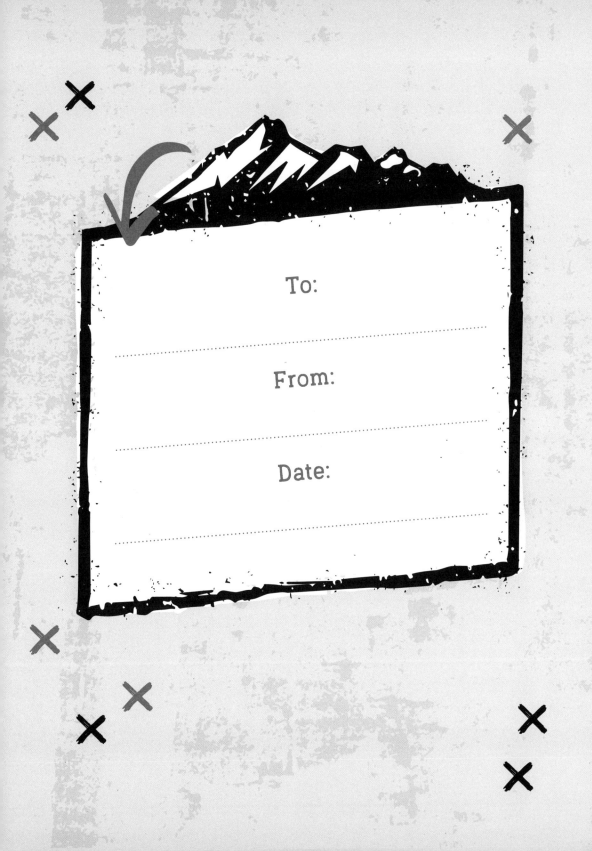

To:

From:

Date:

# You Are

## ADVENTUROUS

### and

## BRAVE

**A DEVOTIONAL SKETCHBOOK
FOR BOYS**

BARBOUR **kidz**
A Division of Barbour Publishing

Published by Barbour Publishing, Inc., 1810 Barbour Drive, Uhrichsville, Ohio 44683, www.barbourbooks.com

*Our mission is to inspire the world with the life-changing message of the Bible.*

 Member of the Evangelical Christian Publishers Association

Printed in China.

000802  0821  HA

# YOU ARE ADVENTUROUS AND BRAVE!

## "Be strong and have strength of heart."
### DEUTERONOMY 31:6

Bravery might be jumping into a river to save someone who's drowning. Or it might be standing up for a classmate who's being bullied. Or it might be staying true to God and His Word when nobody else seems to care.

Those things sound kind of hard, don't they? But the truth is, if you love God—if you follow His Son, Jesus—you can be brave in *every* situation. Why? Because God will give you *His own power* to stand up for the truth, to show love to everyone, and so much more! He'll give you the courage you need to pursue big dreams—the dreams He has given you—to become a strong man of God who looks out for others.

This sketchbook is overflowing with devotional readings and sketch prompts—each one highlighting what God's Word says to you, brave boy! Even if you don't *feel* brave, keep reading—the Bible has the power to give you strength. Whether you're dealing with fear, choices, family, forgiveness, the future, or any other challenges, these devotions and sketch pages will reveal what God's Word has to say. . .helping you to build a foundation of bravery—for life!

# MISUNDERSTOOD KINDNESS

*Love is kind. Love is not jealous. Love does not put
itself up as being important. Love has no pride.*
1 Corinthians 13:4

What do most boys want to be known for? Being smart? Being strong? Being cool? How about being kind?

For many guys, kindness isn't at the top of the list. People who are kind are sometimes thought of as weak or uncool or even simpleminded. But kindness is misunderstood.

It's easy to be mean to someone who is different from you—but kindness requires strength. Being kind when others aren't might seem like an uncool choice, but Jesus doesn't care what other people think about you. He cares what *you* think about *Him*—and wants you to show His love to others, whether that's considered cool or not. Because Jesus commands it, being kind is the smartest choice.

Are you brave enough, strong enough, and smart enough to choose kindness? Even if you honestly answer "no," God is kind enough to give you the help you need. Just ask!

Lord, please give me the courage, strength,
and wisdom I need to be kind today—especially
when people around me are being mean.

Draw a picture below that
shows an act of kindness.

## THINK ABOUT IT!
What can you do to show someone kindness today?

# POWER UP

*"But you will receive power when the Holy Spirit comes into your life. You will tell about Me in the city of Jerusalem and over all the countries of Judea and Samaria and to the ends of the earth."*

ACTS 1:8

If you like superhero stories, you probably know how many of them got their superpowers. The Green Lantern has a special ring, Spider-Man was bitten by a radioactive bug, and the Hulk was exposed to gamma radiation.

When we accept Jesus as our Savior, He give us the gift of eternal life. But He also gives us the power of the Holy Spirit. The Spirit then gives us all the power we need to do Jesus' work on earth. When we follow the Holy Spirit's leading, we become God's champions by spreading His gift of salvation through Jesus.

It might be scary to tell another person about Jesus. You don't know if they'll be excited or maybe make fun of you. The good news is that when we do God's work, *He* provides the help we need—through the powerful gift of the Holy Spirit!

Father, teach me to listen to
Your Spirit as I live each day.

Draw your favorite superhero.

## THINK ABOUT IT!
What qualities make a superhero "super"?

# DON'T BE AFRAID

*When he saw the angel,
Zacharias was troubled and afraid.*
Luke 1:12

Have you ever had a dream that made you wake up in fear? Then you probably know how Zacharias felt. He had never met an angel before, but suddenly there was one right in front of him—and Zacharias *wasn't* dreaming.

He might have been breathing fast, sweating, or looking for a way out. Zacharias was too scared to think straight, too frightened to listen well—even though the angel had good news to share.

You've been scared at times, haven't you? We all have. But no matter how frightened we are, God is always with us. And He doesn't want us to live our lives in fear.

We can't just stop being afraid on our own. We will need help, just like Zacharias did. The angel told him, "Do not be afraid," and explained that God had heard his prayers for a son. Even better, God was going to answer them!

There's no trouble God can't handle, and nothing scares Him. Why should anything scare us?

Lord, I have been scared and didn't even ask
You for help. Next time, make me remember You.

Draw a picture of you conquering your biggest fear.

## THINK ABOUT IT!
When you know Jesus, how is it possible
to NOT be afraid of anything?

# LEARN, TRUST, SHARE

*So then, faith comes to us by hearing the Good News.
And the Good News comes by someone preaching it.*
ROMANS 10:17

How do you learn things? If you're at school, you listen to the teacher in the front of the classroom. Some people watch online tutorials. Many people learn by reading books.

Whatever the method, the learning *process* is basically the same. First, someone has to share information with you. Second, you trust that what you've learned is true, and make it part of your life. Third, when you have learned something good, you probably want to share it.

Faith works the same way. Someone helped you realize that you are a sinner in need of a Savior. They told you about Jesus and His sacrifice on the cross so you could be right with God. You trusted Jesus for salvation. Now you should want to share it with others.

God's love is for everyone, but not everyone has heard the message yet. Who will you share the good news with today?

Lord, please give me courage to share the
good news of Your love with someone today.

Sketch a picture of someone in
your life who needs to know Jesus.

## THINK ABOUT IT!

When God gives you an opportunity to share Jesus
with another kid (or even an adult), what will you say?

# WAIT FOR IT. . .

*"I wait for Your saving power, O Lord."*
GENESIS 49:18

Sometimes waiting is really hard. Do you like waiting for Christmas morning? How about the last day of school? Or your family's vacation to the beach? All of us struggle to wait for exciting things.

But patience is very important. For one thing, you can't make time go any faster, so impatience will just make you miserable. And if you try to rush ahead of *God's* timing for something, you can really mess up your life.

Kids often want to go places, see things, and have stuff that they really aren't ready for. That's why God tells parents to train and protect their kids. If they say "no" and you get frustrated (and it happens to everyone), step back and take a deep breath. Don't try to be too grown-up, too fast . . .trust your parents to know what's best for you and when.

In a way, that's God's "saving power" in your life. Wait for it—someday, you'll be glad you did.

Heavenly Father, please help me to be patient,
in good times and especially in the difficult ones.

Draw a picture of something you're waiting for right now.

## THINK ABOUT IT!
Why is patience so important?

# NO-WORRY BIRDS

*"Look at the birds. They do not plant seeds. They do not gather grain. They have no grain buildings for keeping grain. Yet God feeds them. Are you not worth more than the birds?"*

LUKE 12:24

Imagine a flock of "farming fowl"—birds that hoe the ground, plant seeds, and operate bird-sized tractors to harvest their grain. Would they wear overalls? Would they go to farm shows to learn all the latest research? Would they worry over the weather forecast?

Actually, birds just fly from one meal to the next, finding food pretty much wherever they turn. They leave the farming to someone else. Who is that? Well, *God!*

And you know what God said about the birds? That you're worth more than they are. If God said it, you know it's true. And if He takes care of those birds—billions and billions of them, all over the world—then He can take care of You. In fact, He's done that every day of your life.

So, what are you worried about? If God's handling everything, there are better ways to spend your time—like telling Him "thanks."

Father, please help me to be grateful rather than anxious.

Sketch a picture of something you're thankful for.

## THINK ABOUT IT!
In what ways can you show God that you're grateful?

# GOD'S MESSAGE

*No part of the Holy Writings came long ago because of what man wanted to write. But holy men who belonged to God spoke what the Holy Spirit told them.*

2 PETER 1:21

The Bible is more than just a book—it's really a collection of books. It's like sixty-six books all glued together under one cover.

Did you know that around forty people wrote the Bible? The authors include familiar names like Moses, Daniel, Isaiah, Matthew, and Paul—and some less famous guys like Obadiah and Habakkuk. They wrote from different times and places, but they each had one very important thing in common: God's Holy Spirit told them what to say.

It's true! When you read the Bible, you're reading exactly what God wants you to know. The Bible isn't just the ideas of men—it's the perfect, powerful truth of God. It's the life-changing invitation that welcomes us into God's family. It's the wise and good and hopeful message that lets us live with courage in a crazy world.

The Bible is God's message to people—to *you*. Make sure you know what it says.

Lord, please help me to read and understand Your Word.

Draw a picture of your favorite Bible story.

## THINK ABOUT IT!
Why is it important to read the Bible?

# BETTER TO OBEY

*Samuel said, "Is the Lord pleased as much with burnt gifts as He is when He is obeyed? See, it is better to obey than to give gifts."*
1 Samuel 15:22

Jesus was brave when He made sure to do everything His Father asked Him to do. To be a brave boy means you will work on living each day like Jesus did.

Sometimes it's hard to do what you're told. Imagine you didn't get enough sleep, but your parent is telling you to hurry up and get ready for school. Obeying like Jesus means you act respectfully, getting ready without an attitude.

Remember Adam and Eve? They show what happens when we *don't* obey. God gave them a beautiful home in Eden, but they disobeyed His one simple rule. Then they had to leave paradise and find a new home that wasn't nearly as nice. Pretty sad, huh?

Whatever the situation, the best gift you can give yourself is to obey God. Yeah, sometimes that's tough—but don't forget that He'll help you do whatever He wants you to do!

Lord, please help me to obey Your commands.
I want to live in a way that pleases You.

# Draw a picture that illustrates obeying.

## THINK ABOUT IT!
Why is obeying so hard?

# STICK AROUND

*A friend loves at all times.*
PROVERBS 17:17

Losing friends is never fun, but it happens sometimes.

You've probably lost friends for silly reasons. Maybe they got mad at you because they were jealous about something. Or maybe they heard some gossip about you and believed it—without talking to you first.

God wants you to be a different kind of friend. He wants you to be the kind of guy who sticks around when everyone else is leaving, even when your friend messes up. Especially when he messes up. Why? Because that's the type of friend Jesus is to you.

Sometimes you disobey your parents. Sometimes you think more about yourself than others. And sometimes you tell lies. But Jesus always forgives you when you ask. That's called "grace."

Be a "grace-full" friend to others. It's a great way to witness to those who don't yet know Jesus. And for those who do know Him, it's a great reminder of the love God shows us through Jesus.

We all make mistakes. Let's all stick around for each other.

Lord, I want to be the type of person
who loves my friends at all times.

Sketch a picture of your favorite friend.

## THINK ABOUT IT!
What things can you do to be a good friend?

# EMOTIONS ARE OKAY

*Then Jesus cried.*
JOHN 11:35

Boys and girls are different—that's just the way God made us. Though our bodies have a lot of similarities, they're not exactly alike. And, in general, the way we think and feel is different too. Girls are usually more emotional than boys.

But that doesn't mean boys can't or shouldn't show emotions. Even Jesus cried after one of His good friends, a man named Lazarus, had died. If Jesus could show that kind of emotion in public, don't you think we can too?

Besides sadness, Jesus expressed emotions like love, anger, compassion, frustration, and everything else people feel. Even though He was God, He was also completely human—and He felt all the same emotions we do. He just kept everything in a perfect balance.

Jesus' example is what we need to aim for. We can get too emotional, whether we're overly angry or we can't stop crying. So we should ask God to help us manage our emotions. He is always glad to make us more like Jesus.

Father, please strengthen me when I'm too weak and soften me when I'm too tough. Make my emotions like those of Jesus.

Draw a picture of something that makes you happy.

## THINK ABOUT IT!
Why is it important to be in control of your emotions?

# PRAY INSTEAD

*Do not worry. Learn to pray about everything.*
*Give thanks to God as you ask Him for what you need.*
PHILIPPIANS 4:6

Do you know the story of Chicken Little? One day an acorn falls from a tree, hitting Mr. Little on the head. Surprised, he quickly convinces himself that it was actually the *sky* that struck him. He runs about screaming, "The sky is falling! The sky is falling!"

That's a silly response, right? But we all experience "falling sky" moments at times. It may be at home, or at school, or with friends—something happens that makes us want to panic. When you feel fear, stop and pray. Praying can calm you down, because you'll remember who is in control of everything. . .God.

Jesus once said, "Look at the birds in the sky. They do not plant seeds. They do not gather grain. They do not put grain into a building to keep. Yet your Father in heaven feeds them! Are you not more important than the birds?" (Matthew 6:26).

Well, yes you are. Don't be a Chicken Little, or a little chicken. Instead, pray.

Father, when I am worried, help me to trust You.

Draw a picture of Chicken Little.

## THINK ABOUT IT!
How does it make you feel to know that
God is in control of everything?

# RESCUE THE FEARFUL

*But when [Peter] saw the strong wind, he was afraid.*
*He began to go down in the water. He cried out, "Lord, save me!"*
MATTHEW 14:30

When we learn to swim, we all love a good floatie. They hold us up in the pool and make us feel brave while we splash in the water. We're confident when we can enjoy the water while still breathing good air.

It wasn't quite that way for Peter.

Peter watched Jesus walk on the water, and he wanted to do that too. But Peter didn't have a floatie—instead, he had Jesus, who was more than enough. When Peter trusted Jesus, he breathed good air with every miracle step he took. When Peter began to doubt, he sank. He needed help, and Jesus came to the rescue.

When you're in trouble, you know who to ask. You know that Jesus *wants* to help you out.

So walk with Him and feel brave. Trust Him and enjoy confidence. Follow Him and discover the very best adventures.

Lord Jesus, I will always need Your help. I need Your rescue.
When I'm worried, You're the One I need to talk to most.

Sketch a picture of Jesus and Peter walking on the water.

## THINK ABOUT IT!
What should you do when you're afraid or full of doubt?

# JOYFUL GIVING

*They said to Moses, "The people are bringing much more
than enough for the work the Lord told us to do."*
EXODUS 36:5

Moses told the people of Israel that God wanted them to build a meeting tent, also known as "the tabernacle." That was where God would meet with His people as they traveled through the desert on the way to the Promised Land. Moses asked the people to bring gold, silver and brass, different colors of cloth, animal skins, perfume, and other things as gifts to the Lord.

Guess what? They brought so many gifts that Moses told the people to stop! What would happen in the church today if all God's people responded so generously? How many homeless people would be fed? How many needy children might get clothes? How many houses could be built?

Does this story reflect *your* attitude about giving to God? Are you willing to give so much that every need is met? Would you like to make your pastor tell the members of your church to stop giving for a while?

Lord, give me a joyful heart—one that can't wait to
give You my tithes and offerings each week.

Draw a picture of something you could
give away to a person in need.

## THINK ABOUT IT!
How does it feel when you share your stuff with someone else?

# FRUSTRATING AND UNFAIR

*Joseph's brothers were jealous of him.*
GENESIS 37:11

Joseph had ten older brothers, and they were all jealous of him. When he told them he'd dreamed that they were bowing down to him, they were furious—and they plotted a whole bunch of trouble. You can read the whole story in Genesis 37–50. In a nutshell, the brothers sold Joseph as a slave, but years later he became as the second most powerful leader in Egypt. Crazy, huh?

Well, not when you consider that "the Lord was with Joseph" (Genesis 39:2). Through every frustrating and unfair thing that Joseph went through, God was there. And God was working out every detail for His much bigger purposes.

He does that in our lives too. As the apostle Paul wrote, "We know that God makes all things work together for the good of those who love Him and are chosen to be a part of His plan" (Romans 8:28).

God knows every tough thing you face, and He's ready to make something good out of them. Your job is just to stay faithful.

Lord God, please help me to stay faithful
when life seem frustrating and unfair.

Read Joseph's story in your Bible and then
draw a picture of his colorful coat.

## THINK ABOUT IT!
Has there been a time in your life when God
made something good from a bad situation?

# THE WAY OF LIFE

*You will show me the way of life. Being with You is to be full of joy. In Your right hand there is happiness forever.*
PSALM 16:11

People who don't know Jesus spend their time and energy trying to discover meaning in life. Many times, they seek happiness in sinful ways and never really find lasting joy. But Jesus calls His followers to a different kind of life. He said, "My sheep hear My voice and I know them. They follow Me" (John 10:27). Jesus' sheep follow Him into eternal life.

The world says right now is all that matters. Christians live with heaven in mind. The world says you should seek joy in whatever makes you happy. Christians find joy in the Lord. The world says you have to look out for yourself. Christians know that nothing can touch them unless Jesus allows it.

Are you living with heaven in mind? Are you finding joy in the Lord? Are you trusting in the Lord for protection? If so, you have found the way of life.

Lord, I thank You for showing me the way of life!
May I never stray from Your path.

Draw a picture of sheep following Jesus.

## THINK ABOUT IT!
What makes Jesus trustworthy?

# DO CHORES LIKE JESUS

*"I have done this to show you what should be done.
You should do as I have done to you."*

JOHN 13:15

Imagine that you are a servant in Bible times. You're working in a big house in Jerusalem. To your surprise, that popular teacher Jesus comes into the house. He goes to an upper room to eat supper with His twelve apostles.

Usually a servant would wash the feet of each guest. But Jesus, smiling, takes the water bowl and towel from your hands, telling you that you're free to go do other things. You start to leave, but curiosity gets the best of you. When you turn around, you see that Jesus has knelt down and is washing an apostle's dirty feet. You can't believe it.

In today's verse, Jesus tells you to serve others. That includes doing everyday chores, even unpleasant ones. It also includes doing jobs *before* you're asked. What chore do you need to do now? Clean your room? Take out the garbage? Wash the dishes?

Father God, Jesus was more than willing to wash
twenty-four stinky feet. Would You please help
me to do my chores happily, like Jesus did?

Sketch a picture of your least favorite chore.

## THINK ABOUT IT!
Why do you think Jesus wants you to serve others?

# DO WHAT GOD SAYS

*"Not everyone who says to me, 'Lord, Lord,' will go into the holy nation of heaven. The one who does the things My Father in heaven wants him to do will go into the holy nation of heaven."*
MATTHEW 7:21

Becoming braver each day means obeying God—the first time, every time. It's easy to think we know better, but we really don't. We need to admit that only God knows everything.

Moses learned this lesson after God spoke to him through a burning bush (see Exodus 3). God said Moses would lead the Israelites out of their slavery in Egypt. But Moses couldn't believe it, and he started making excuses instead of obeying. "Who am I to lead the people?" he asked.

It took a long time—years in fact—before Moses did what God had told him to do: lead the Israelites out of their slavery. We can only imagine what would have happened had Moses obeyed God the first time.

Practice obeying God the first time, every time, even when it's hard. Then watch what great things He'll do through you!

Lord, please help me obey Your laws the first time, every time!

Draw a picture of Moses and the burning bush.

## THINK ABOUT IT!
What happens when you make excuses instead of obeying?

# SIBLING RIVALRY

*Martha was working hard getting the supper ready.*
*She came to Jesus and said, "Do You see that my*
*sister is not helping me? Tell her to help me."*
LUKE 10:40

Sometimes the hardest people to get along with are members of our own family. We know more about them than anyone else—anyone but God. Family members know just the right words to make us mad, but they also know what we like. . .and might surprise us in ways that bring a smile.

Maybe you've heard the phrase "sibling rivalry"—that happens when two or more children in the same family just can't seem to get along. It happens, but it was never God's plan.

Jesus saw sibling rivalry up close with two sisters. When Mary didn't help out with the meal, Martha told Jesus to make her help.

Family can be a real learning experience, and brave boys make the best of it. How do you learn to get along? Speak kindly. Offer to help. Ignore careless comments. Forgive.

In time, you'll replace rivalry with respect. . .maybe even love.

Lord, I know that family is important to You. . .
so please make it important to me.

# Sketch a picture of your family.

# THINK ABOUT IT!
What do you need to change in order to get
along better with your family members?

# LOVE GOD, OTHERS. . .AND ANIMALS

*Jesus said to Peter the second time, "Simon, son of John,
do you love Me?" He answered Jesus, "Yes, Lord, You know
that I love You." Jesus said to him, "Take care of My sheep."*

JOHN 21:16

When Dan was eleven years old, his parents let him buy two lambs. Dan and his older brother made a circular wire fence that stood up on its own. It didn't need any fence posts, so Dan could move the enclosure—and the sheep—around the lawn. Those sheep loved to eat the grass, so Dan didn't have to mow the yard anymore. He just had to take very good care of the sheep day after day.

So what does that have to do with loving God? Well, bad things happen when an animal runs out of food or water. And bad things happen when you neglect the people God's put into your life. When you care for others—whether they're animals or other people—you're showing your love for Jesus. Take care of His sheep!

Lord, I thank You that I can show my love
for You by caring for others—even pets.

# Draw a picture of your pet.

## THINK ABOUT IT!
What would happen if you stopped
taking care of your family pet?

# GOD'S GOT THIS!

*But Moses said to the people, "Do not be afraid!*
*Be strong, and see how the Lord will save you*
*today. For the Egyptians you have seen*
*today, you will never see again."*
EXODUS 14:13

Do you remember the story of "the Exodus"—the time God's people escaped their slavery in Egypt? Moses led the Israelites out of the country, to the edge of the Red Sea. But how would they get across. . .especially with Egyptian soldiers chasing them down?

The Israelites waited by the water's edge just as God had told them to. They were afraid when they saw the soldiers coming closer. But Moses said God would fight for them. He would save the people in a way they couldn't even imagine.

That's when Moses lifted up his walking stick. The sea split in two. The people walked through on dry ground. The Egyptians rode into the sea after the Israelites, and the waters rushed back into place. Every soldier was drowned, and God's people were saved.

God can do similar things for you today. Stay positive. Don't worry. He's got this!

Lord God, help me to never worry and
instead trust Your goodness and power.

Draw a picture that shows how Moses and the Israelites crossed the Red Sea.

## THINK ABOUT IT!
What is something that you're trusting God with today?

# HELPING GOD BY HELPING OTHERS

*Religion that is pure and good before God the Father is to help children who have no parents and to care for women whose husbands have died who have troubles.*

JAMES 1:27

When you know of someone in need, it's easy to think, *Someone should help them!* Maybe that "someone" is you.

It's normal to feel bad when you see a lonely kid or an older lady who lives by herself. But God doesn't just want us to feel bad—He wants us to do something. He wants us to "care for" people like that.

To do this, you'll need courage from God and maybe some help from your parents. If it's okay with them, invite a lonely kid over for dinner. Or offer to mow grass or take out the trash for a single lady down the street.

Lots of people could use a friend. Maybe God is calling you to be that friend to the needy people of your neighborhood. It's been said that Christians are Jesus' hands and feet on earth today. By helping others, you help God.

Father, please help me show Your love by encouraging sad and lonely people.

Draw a picture that shows you being
the hands and feet of Jesus.

## THINK ABOUT IT!
What does it mean that when you
help others, you're helping God?

# TRUTH BRINGS PEACE

*"These are the things you are to do: Speak the truth to one another.
Judge with truth so there will be peace within your gates."*
ZECHARIAH 8:16

In Old Testament times—that is, in the centuries before Jesus was born—God's people made a lot of mistakes. A lot of big mistakes, even things like worshipping false gods. God gave them many chances to do the right thing, but they refused. Finally, God punished them by allowing invaders to wreck their country.

But God always loved His people, and through the prophet Zechariah He said that He would restore the country and its capital city, Jerusalem. God had many blessings in mind for the people, but they had to do what He wanted them to do. And what He wanted was in today's verse: they had to speak and judge truthfully. When they did that, God promised the people "peace within your gates."

In our world, some people hate the truth. It doesn't automatically bring peace. But among real Christians, truth and honesty are expected and appreciated. Speak the truth to one another!

Father, help me always to be truthful when I speak.

Sketch a picture of something peaceful.

## THINK ABOUT IT!
Why is speaking the truth so important?

# NOT WISHFUL THINKING

*Now faith is being sure we will get what we hope for.
It is being sure of what we cannot see. God was pleased
with the men who had faith who lived long ago.*

HEBREWS 11:1–2

Imagine it's your birthday. You're about to blow out the candles when someone shouts, "Make a wish!"

Some people think faith is like believing a birthday wish will come true—but that's really called "wishful thinking." Faith is knowing *without a doubt* the all-powerful, truthful God will do what He said He would do.

What are some of God's promises you can believe in? Well, He promises to forgive you if you confess your sins (1 John 1:9), to give wisdom when you ask for it (James 1:5), and to give you eternal life if you believe in Jesus as your Savior (John 3:16). He commands you to be strong and courageous because He will be with you wherever you go (Joshua 1:9).

When you believe God will keep His promises, He will be pleased at your faith in Him. That's a brave way to live.

Lord, You keep Your promises.
Help me to claim them and live by faith in You.

Draw a picture of something you've wished for.

## THINK ABOUT IT!
What is the difference between
making a wish and having faith?

# MONEY!

*"After a long time the owner of those servants came back. He wanted to know what had been done with his money. The one who had received the five pieces of money worth much came and handed him five pieces more. He said, 'Sir, you gave me five pieces of money. See! I used it and made five more pieces.'"*
MATTHEW 25:19-20

Many guys dream of making money. They hope to play in the NBA, lead a big company, or star in blockbuster movies. . .and make millions along the way.

The Bible says, "the love of money is the beginning of all kinds of sin" (1 Timothy 6:10). But notice that it's "the *love* of money," not money itself, that causes trouble. God encourages people to work hard and earn an honest living. As you earn more and more, you'll have more and more to give to people who need help.

Whether you're mowing lawns for a few dollars a week or your rich great-grandfather left you a zillion dollars, be wise. Ask God to help you handle your money—because it really came from Him anyway.

Lord, may I stand out from this world by not loving money.

Sketch a picture of you in your future career.

## THINK ABOUT IT!
What are some good ways you can manage your money?

# YOUR GOD, MY GOD

*But Ruth said, "Do not beg me to leave you or turn away from following you. I will go where you go. I will live where you live. Your people will be my people. And your God will be my God."*
RUTH 1:16

You probably have someone you look up to. It could be your dad, your mom, a grandparent, or even a teacher. You pay attention to the way they do things. What they think is important to you. You want to do what they do.

In the Bible, a woman named Ruth loved her mother-in-law. Ruth wanted to follow Naomi wherever she went. . .and Naomi wanted to move back to the place where she was born, Bethlehem. So Ruth made the choice to follow Naomi.

You can make the choice to follow God.

Ruth made the choice to love Naomi.

You can make the choice to love God.

Ruth is remembered for her wise choices.

You can be remembered that way too. Make Naomi and Ruth's God your God.

Heavenly Father, I want to make my home with You and be part of Your family. I want You to be my God.

Draw a picture that shows you doing something wise.

## THINK ABOUT IT!

Think about a wise decision you've made, and then think
about an unwise decision you've made. What were
the results of your decisions and why?

# ASKING FOR GIFTS

*"You are bad and you know how to give good things to your children. How much more will your Father in heaven give good things to those who ask Him?"*

MATTHEW 7:11

Kids always ask a parent or guardian or favorite aunt for special things. We want an ice cream cone or a new shirt or a cool book we saw at the store. Adults don't always give us what we want, but many times they do. They like to be generous and make us happy.

Jesus said God the Father is the same way—if we ask for "good things." Of course, it's possible to ask for bad things, things that might hurt us or interfere with other people's well-being. But if we ask God for wisdom, strength, and maybe even money for helping others, He's going to be like the adults in our lives. . .happy to give.

Sometimes God will say *no* to our requests. He knows there are times we might misuse what we ask for. But if you see needs you'd like to help with, ask God to provide. He gives good things!

Lord, please give me what I need for helping others.

Draw a picture of something you needed that God provided.

## THINK ABOUT IT!
What is the difference between a need and a want?

# LEARNING THE HARD WAY

*Jesus said to them, "My mother and brothers*
*are these who hear the Word of God and do it."*
LUKE 8:21

Jesus said you're an important part of His family when you hear *and obey* God's Word. Jonah learned that lesson the hard way.

God had called Jonah to preach in the big, scary city of Nineveh. Jonah thought, *No way!* But God loved those wicked, violent people and wanted them to be saved.

Jonah not only disobeyed God, he ran in the *opposite* direction. But while he was on his getaway ship, a huge storm blew up. Jonah realized God was getting his attention.

You probably know the story: Jonah jumped overboard and was swallowed by a giant fish. He spent three days in the fish's stomach before being spit out on shore—and then he finally obeyed God by preaching in Nineveh.

It was a tough lesson, but there was a happy ending: many people were saved when Jonah did what God said.

Lord, please help me to study Your Word and do what it says!

Draw a picture from the story of Jonah and the whale.

## THINK ABOUT IT!
What could Jonah have done differently
to avoid his encounter with the whale?

# KEEP YOUR FAMILY FRIENDS

*Do not leave your own friend or your father's friend alone.*
PROVERBS 27:10

King Solomon had a friend named Hiram, the king of Tyre. Hiram had also been friends with Solomon's dad, King David. When Solomon began to build God's temple in Jerusalem, he asked Hiram to supply the lumber and some of his workers. Hiram was happy to help. You can read about this in 1 Kings 5.

Sadly, when Solomon's son Rehoboam became king, he didn't value this family friendship. Instead, 1 Kings 12:8, says, "Rehoboam turned away from the wise words the leaders [who worked with his father] gave him. Instead he spoke with the young men who grew up with him and stood by him." He ended up losing his kingdom.

Do your parents have long-time friends who've always seemed to be there for your family? As you grow up, don't leave those friends behind. They will always be happy to help you and give you advice. You can certainly make your own friends, but your parents' friends are important too. Honor them and see how God can use them in your life.

God, I thank You for giving my family good friends.

Sketch a picture of a friend who's like family to you.

## THINK ABOUT IT!
What things make a friend feel like family?

# IMPOSSIBLE PROBLEMS

*One of His followers was Andrew, Simon Peter's brother. He said to Jesus, "There is a boy here who has five loaves of barley bread and two small fish. What is that for so many people?"*

JOHN 6:8-9

When you're faced with a big problem, you may be tempted to give up before you begin. Jesus' disciples did that when He asked them to get food for thousands of hungry people.

One disciple spoke up to say they didn't have enough money to feed a crowd that large. Andrew, another disciple, found a boy with five loaves of bread and two small fish—but he knew it wasn't possible to feed everyone with that.

Jesus *loves* impossible situations, though—because they allow Him to show His power. When the boy offered up his lunch, Jesus gave thanks to God the Father and started handing out bread and fish, bread and fish, bread and fish to the crowd. In the end, everyone ate as much as they wanted. . .and there were twelve baskets left over!

When a problem feels impossible, give it to Jesus and watch Him work.

Lord, show me that all things are possible with You.

Draw a picture of the simple meal that Jesus used
to feed thousands of hungry people.

## THINK ABOUT IT!
Do you have a problem that seems impossible?
What should you do about it?

# HOW TO LOOK FOR GOD

*Look for the Lord and His strength. Look for His face all the time.*
PSALM 105:4

If you wanted to see the Lord's face today, where would you look? Well, you could open your Bible to Psalm 105 and find that the verse after today's scripture says, "Remember the great and powerful works that He has done. Keep in mind what He has decided and told us" (Psalm 105:5).

In other words, if you want to see the Lord's face today, you can look at nature. No, nature isn't God! But the Lord God made heaven and earth. (You can read that in the very first verse of the Bible.) When you look at nature, then you can see what God is like.

First, nature tells us that the Lord God is amazingly powerful. Second, He has created untold billions of interesting things for us to see—on land, in the ocean, and overhead in the sky. Best of all? He gives us those things to enjoy!

Lord, when I see the amazing things You have made, I feel like saying, "Wow!" Thank You for giving us such an incredible world.

**Draw a picture of your favorite thing in nature.**

## THINK ABOUT IT!
What can nature tell us about God?

# THE BEST TRANSLATOR

*In the same way, the Holy Spirit helps us where we are weak.*
*We do not know how to pray or what we should pray for, but the Holy*
*Spirit prays to God for us with sounds that cannot be put into words.*
ROMANS 8:26

Have you heard of Dr. Dolittle? He's a character in a series of children's books, a veterinarian who can understand and speak the language of any animal he meets. Wouldn't that be an amazing skill to have?

Animals in the Dr. Dolittle stories need a translator because they can't tell human beings what they're feeling. In some ways, the Holy Spirit does the same work between us and God. When you struggle to pray—when nothing comes to mind or it's hard to concentrate—the Holy Spirit helps out. He "translates" our prayers to God in the exact way we meant to say them.

If you don't know what to pray for or feel like you might have said the wrong thing in a prayer, don't be discouraged. Thanks to the Holy Spirit, God hears your prayers perfectly. Just keep praying!

God, I thank You for Your Holy Spirit's help in prayer.

Sketch your favorite animal.

## THINK ABOUT IT!
When was the last time you talked to God?
What do you need to share with Him today?

# THE LOVE RESPONSE

*"I say to you who hear Me, love those who work against you.
Do good to those who hate you. Respect and give thanks for those who
try to bring bad to you. Pray for those who make it very hard for you."*
LUKE 6:27–28

Jesus spoke about the worst things people do, then told you how to respond. When other people work hard to keep you from achieving your goals, love them. When people hate you, do good in return. When they try to get you in trouble, give thanks. When they make life difficult, pray for them.

Who could do that? It sounds impossible.

Well, Jesus didn't ask you to do something that had never been done before. *He* loved, *He* did good, *He* gave thanks, and *He* prayed when He was betrayed, hurt, and killed. Now He wants you to do what He did when people were against Him.

Ask Jesus for help and follow His example. Show His "love response" to everyone.

Lord, this seems so hard—but You loved those who hated
You. Help me, and I will do my best to show Your love.

Draw a picture of Jesus showing love to someone.

## THINK ABOUT IT!
What are some ways you can love like Jesus?

# THE GREAT HOPE

*We are to be looking for the great hope and the coming of
our great God and the One Who saves, Christ Jesus.*

TITUS 2:13

Have you ever looked forward to a special event? Maybe you couldn't wait to ride the roller coasters at your favorite amusement park. Or maybe you were eager to see your school friends at a classmate's birthday party. Maybe you were itching to play in your team's big game. Anticipating something makes it even more enjoyable when the event actually happens.

The same is true in our Christian lives. In today's verse, the apostle Paul says we should be looking for the "great hope"—Jesus' second coming to earth. Galatians 5:5 mentions this great hope as well, and gives us a clearer understanding of what it means: "We are waiting for the hope of being made right with God. This will come through the Holy Spirit and by faith."

When Jesus returns to earth, He's going to make everything right. Sadness, sickness, death—all of those things will be finished! So go ahead and think about your own special events. But spend even more time thinking about Jesus' return.

Come, Lord Jesus.

Sketch a picture of an event you're looking forward to.

## THINK ABOUT IT!
Why should we be looking forward to Jesus' return?

# GOODBYE, LAZINESS

*When men are lazy, the roof begins to fall in.*
*When they will do no work, the rain comes into the house.*
ECCLESIASTES 10:18

When people work out at the gym, they get stronger and healthier. It's the same with your spiritual life. If you read your Bible and talk to God every day, you build stronger spiritual muscles. Those "exercises" help keep your thoughts focused on truth. When we're lazy spiritually, we run the risk of wandering away from God. And where we end up, nothing good happens.

The Bible often warns against laziness. We're told that we should imitate the hardworking ants (Proverbs 6:6-8), that laziness leads to being poor (Proverbs 6:1-11), and that people who won't work shouldn't be given food (2 Thessalonians 3:10). And today's verse shows that laziness leads to bigger problems—like the roof of your house collapsing!

Decide today to say goodbye to laziness. With God's strength, you can work hard and bring Him glory.

Lord Jesus, it's easy for me to get lazy and not give my best effort. Help me to work hard at everything I do, whether that's mowing the grass or studying Your Word.

# Draw a picture that shows you working hard.

## THINK ABOUT IT!
What is the different between being physically lazy and spiritually lazy?

# KING OF THE JUNGLE?

*There is hope for the one who is among the living.*
*For sure a live dog is better off than a dead lion.*
ECCLESIASTES 9:4

Whether or not you've taken a safari to Africa, you've seen lions—maybe in a zoo, or on TV, or pictured in a book. Lions are impressive, and we'd all like to be as strong and confident as they are.

But even "the king of the jungle" has his limits. The Bible says that a dead lion is no better than any live dog. (Imagine a shivering poodle!) That's because with life, there's hope. No matter how weak we might feel, God can make us strong. No matter how confused we are, God can give us wisdom. No matter how tough things seem, God will always be with us.

You don't have to be the strongest, most confident guy in your school, or neighborhood, or world. Just know that God's strength and confidence are yours whenever you need them. All you have to do is ask.

Father, I'm thankful that I don't have to be "king of the jungle." May I always remember that You are the King of the universe.

Draw a picture of the king of the jungle.

## THINK ABOUT IT!

Have you ever asked God for strength and confidence?
What happened after you asked?

# SOLID FOUNDATION

*Trust in the Lord forever.*
*For the Lord God is a Rock that lasts forever.*
ISAIAH 26:4

Have you ever seen a new building under construction? The first thing to "go up" is actually "way down"—the foundation. Machines dig out a trench that's filled with heavy-duty concrete. When that's rock hard, the rest of the house can be built on top of it. Without a solid foundation, the building would eventually wobble and fall down.

The Bible says God is a rock. He's like a strong, unmoving foundation that you can build your life on. Other people chase money and fame and fun—things that don't last forever and can't save your soul. But brave boys know that life is all about God. When you read His Word, learn His ways, and choose to follow His plan, you are building a solid life that will stand forever. You won't wobble and fall down when hard times come.

The world will tell you to build on other foundations, but they're all like sand on a seashore. Settle yourself on the Rock—God—and you'll never be sorry.

Lord, may I put into practice everything I learn in Your Word.

Draw a building with a strong foundation.

## THINK ABOUT IT!
How is God like a rock?

# WAITING ON THE PROMISE

*Abraham was willing to wait and God
gave to him what He had promised.*
Hebrews 6:15

Did you ever have to wait a long time for something you really wanted? Well, Abraham had to wait *a hundred years* to have his son Isaac. Can you imagine? God promised to give Abraham a child—and because God promised, Abraham waited. Patiently.

The truth is, waiting for things that seem really far away is tough. It's safe to assume that Abraham sometimes struggled with waiting because he really wanted to be a dad! But when God says He'll do something, He does it. . .and it's awesome.

Just as God promised Abraham a son, He promised everyone that He would send His own son to save us—and He did. Then He promised that His Son would come again to take His followers home to heaven—and you can be sure He will.

God didn't say exactly *when* Jesus will come to get us, but He does tell us to wait patiently. That day is going to be incredible!

Dear Lord, help me to remember that Your
promises are worth waiting for. Amen.

Draw a picture of Abraham and his son, Isaac.

## THINK ABOUT IT!

Have you ever had to wait a super-duper long time for something to happen? What was it, and was the wait hard or easy?

# YOUR SUPERPOWER

*Every child of God has power over the sins of the world.*
*The way we have power over the sins of the world is by our faith.*

1 JOHN 5:4

Wouldn't it be cool to have a superpower? It's fun to imagine what life would be like if you could fly or had super strength. But every child of God has a superpower already. Really! By faith, you have power over the sins of the world.

Maybe that doesn't sound like a superpower to you. But just imagine a world free from sin. No one would have to worry about criminals stealing things. There would be no more murder or violence. People would keep their promises and treat everyone else with respect. If that doesn't sound like something a superhero fights for, what does?

God conquered sin when Jesus died on the cross. If you are tempted to do something you shouldn't, ask God for help and He will give you the strength to fight the temptation. You can make this world a better place by using the power God gives you over the sins of the world.

Lord, help me fight off temptation with Your super strength.

Imagine yourself as a superhero.
What would you look like? Draw it here.

## THINK ABOUT IT!
What kinds of things should a superhero fight for?

# PRAISE WHEN SAVED

*Let the people who have been saved say so. He has bought them*
*and set them free from the hand of those who hated them.*
PSALM 107:2

Most everyone knows the story of David and Goliath. A young Israelite—just a shepherd boy—defeats an enormous, experienced Philistine soldier in battle.

But that was only one of the many victories God gave David. As a boy he had defended his flocks of sheep against bears and lions. As a king, he led many successful military efforts. Somehow, in the midst of all his other duties, the poetic and musical David wrote many of the psalms in our Bibles today.

He once sang, "I call to the Lord, Who has the right to be praised. And I am saved from those who hate me" (Psalm 18:3).

Hopefully, we don't have the kind of enemies David did. But when we need help, we should follow his example in calling out to God. Then, after He's helped us, we should tell others what God has done so they can share in our joy.

Father, I thank You for helping me,
no matter what situation I find myself in.

Sketch a picture of David with his sheep.

## THINK ABOUT IT!
How did David defeat the giant, Goliath?
Where did David get his strength?

# ON TARGET

*The children of a young man are like
arrows in the hand of a soldier.*
PSALM 127:4

Have you ever used a bow and arrow? The Bible says you are an arrow. King Solomon, who wrote Psalm 127, might have remembered shooting arrows with his dad, David. He was inspired to use a bow and arrow to talk about brave parents and their boys, and a good future.

Just like soldiers shoot their arrows carefully, parents wisely aim their children. You wouldn't expect a soldier to just pull back the bowstring and zing an arrow into the sky. He carefully aims the arrow, letting it fly only when he has the target in sight.

There should always be a reason for a warrior to shoot an arrow. That's the responsibility God gives moms and dads with their own boys. Parents train their children, aiming them at the target God has set. . .and, at just the right time, send them out on the adventure of life.

God, it's good to know You have a future for me.
Guide me. Guide my family. Help me make the
right choice to go where You send me.

Sketch a picture of an arrow in the center of a bull's-eye.

## THINK ABOUT IT!
How are *you* like an arrow?

# JESUS STILL HEALS TODAY

*Jesus went away from the Jewish place of worship and went into Simon's house. Simon's mother-in-law was in bed, very sick. They asked Jesus to help her. He stood by her and told the disease to leave. It went from her. At once she got up and cared for them.*

LUKE 4:38–39

A lot of us hate being around someone who's sneezing and blowing his nose every two minutes. But Jesus was different. That's right—as God's Son, He could (and still can) heal anyone. And when He was here on earth, He did just that.

Jesus didn't just heal grown-ups like Simon Peter's mother-in-law. He also healed boys and girls who were sick and dying. He even brought a twelve-year-old girl and an older boy back from the dead.

Do you know anyone who is sick? If so, Jesus can use *you*. How? Well, you can pray for that person's healing. The Lord can't wait to hear and answer that kind of prayer—a prayer of strong faith. Go for it!

Lord, I believe You can heal anyone of anything.
Help me to pray in faith for the healing of sick people I know.

Draw a picture of Jesus healing someone who's sick.

## THINK ABOUT IT!
What can you do for someone who's sick today?

# GOD LOVES YOU

*"I say to you, My friends, do not be afraid of those
who kill the body and then can do no more."*
LUKE 12:4

Watching the news can be frightening. Lots of bad things happen every day. Sometimes people get hurt. Sometimes they get killed. That's a good reason to pray, but it's not a good reason to be afraid.

You may not realize it yet, but the time you'll live in this world is pretty short. Someday, though, Christians will live with God forever. Death doesn't stop that from happening. *It can't.*

If you follow Him, Jesus promised to make a home for you in heaven. No one—not popular, angry, or mean people—can take that away. The worst they can do is make life unpleasant here. But when you die, there will be a welcome home party for you in heaven.

Maybe this isn't the easiest thing to think about, but it means that *God loves you.* He cares about you. He looks forward to showing you the home He made for you.

And it's going to be awesome.

Lord, thank You for making a perfect place
where I can be with You forever.

Sketch a picture of what you think heaven might be like.

## THINK ABOUT IT!
What do you think heaven will look like, be like, smell like? . . .

# STICK TO THE BIBLE

*"Do not add to the Word that I tell you, and do not take away
from it. Keep the Laws of the Lord your God which I tell you."*
DEUTERONOMY 4:2

People love new stuff. That's why car companies, phone makers, video
game designers, and movie producers are always advertising "the latest
and greatest." They make a lot of money from people who want new
things.

But here's one thing you should never replace with something new: the
Bible. God gave us His Word so we could know Him and what He wants
for us. And since God never changes, His Word doesn't change either.
As Jesus' friend and follower Peter wrote, "The Word of the Lord will last
forever" (1 Peter 1:25).

Some people don't like what the Bible says so they try to change it.
They add their own thoughts to it. Or they take away parts of the Bible
they don't like. Or they just ignore God's rules entirely. Brave boys, though,
obey God's Word—*every part* of it.

Stick to the Bible, and God will stick with you.

Lord God, please give me the courage to stand with Your Word.

Draw a picture of you reading your Bible in your favorite place.

## THINK ABOUT IT!
Why is it important to obey *all* of God's Word
and not just pieces and parts of it?

# TOMORROW ISN'T CERTAIN

*Do not talk much about tomorrow,*
*for you do not know what a day will bring.*
PROVERBS 27:1

Some people (usually older ones) think a lot about the way things used to be. Other people (usually younger ones) think a lot about tomorrow. But the scriptures tell us to not think too much about either. We can't do anything about the past, and the future isn't in our hands. What we can control are our actions in this minute.

It's so easy to waste time. Video games, YouTube, being lazy. . .sometimes we act as if we have all the time in the world, but we don't really know that. James 4:13-14 says, "Listen! You who say, 'Today or tomorrow we will go to this city and stay a year and make money.' You do not know about tomorrow. What is your life? It is like fog. You see it and soon it is gone."

Brave boys use their time wisely, even when other guys are just fooling around. Set a good example for them—maybe even for the adults around you.

God, help me to make good decisions on how I spend my time.

Sketch a picture of a clock.

## THINK ABOUT IT!
What kinds of things "steal" your time during the day?
How can you better manage your time?

# THE GIFT OF STRENGTH

*I want to see you so I can share some special gift of the
Holy Spirit with you. It will make you strong.*
ROMANS 1:11

You don't have to be naturally courageous to be a brave boy. You just need to allow God's Holy Spirit to work in your life.

The apostle Paul admitted that he wasn't an impressive guy. He once wrote down what other people said about him: "When he is here with us, he is weak and he is hard to listen to" (2 Corinthians 10:10). But you'd have a hard time finding a more courageous man in all of history. He preached the good news about Jesus no matter how many times he was arrested, thrown in jail, beaten, stoned, and shipwrecked. How could he do that?

Only by the gift of the Holy Spirt that made him (and will make *us*) strong.

If you're not super brave, super brainy, or super brawny, that's okay. God will be happy to *give* you whatever power you need to serve Him. Just ask. Then move forward in His strength.

Father, I want the power of Your Holy Spirit.
Please make me strong to do Your work.

Draw a picture of you being super brave.

## THINK ABOUT IT!
Think about someone you know who's courageous.
What kinds of qualities make this person brave?

# THE THINGS YOU NEED

*"Do not worry. Do not keep saying, 'What will we eat?' or, 'What will we drink?' or, 'What will we wear?' The people who do not know God are looking for all these things. Your Father in heaven knows you need all these things."*

MATTHEW 6:31-32

When you're hungry, thirsty, or wondering where you put your favorite shirt, you need to remember this: while so many other people worry about things, God doesn't. He knows what you need. And He wants you to know that there's nothing you worry about that He can't handle.

You probably think about food at least three times a day. (Some boys never stop thinking about food!) You get thirsty several times a day. God made the things you eat and the water you drink. He made the raw materials for the clothes you wear, and the wood and stone that make up the house you live in. He knows what you need, and He provides it. Don't worry!

Father, when I sit down to dinner, drink a bottle of water, or slide a shirt over my head, please help me to worry less and thank You more.

Draw a picture of your favorite food.

## THINK ABOUT IT!
In what ways does God provide what you need?

# BE LIKE NOAH

*Noah did just what God told him to do.*
GENESIS 6:22

One great thing about being obedient is knowing that God is always with you—no matter what. He is there to help you, to guide you, and to remind you to ask forgiveness when you mess up.

Noah obeyed God in a huge way. The Bible says that the world was a very bad place during Noah's lifetime because nobody else wanted to obey God. So the Lord decided to send a flood to wash the world clean. Noah, though, was going to be saved along with his family.

As hard as it was to imagine, Noah believed that God would do as He said. And for the next hundred years, he and his family built the ark. God saved them—and two of every kind of animal—from the great flood.

When we obey the directions He has for us, God gives us daily comfort. Stick with Him! Don't quit. Be patient and watch how God will take your life to awesome places.

Lord God, please help me to listen to Your Word.
Then give me the strength to obey!

Draw a picture of Noah and his ark.

## THINK ABOUT IT!
Do you always do what God asks? Why or why not?

# A TIME TO TAKE CARE

*Anyone who does not take care of his family and those in his house has turned away from the faith. He is worse than a person who has never put his trust in Christ.*

1 TIMOTHY 5:8

God never asks you to do something He doesn't do. He wouldn't ask you to forgive if He never forgave. He wouldn't ask you to love others if He didn't love you. He wouldn't ask you to be kind if He was rude.

These are the attitudes and behaviors He wants you to have in your family.

Family is important—so important that the Bible tells us to take care of each member.

Some families are happy and strong. Others need help. But God is there for every kind of family, and every boy in them.

God is a Father who looks after the needs of His family. If you have a happy home, thank Him for that and make sure you serve everyone well. If your home has problems, pray for God's help. And ask Him to make you forgiving, loving, and kind. . .like Jesus.

Father, You forgive, love, and show kindness.
Help me do that for my family.

Draw a picture of you helping a family member.

## THINK ABOUT IT!
What are some ways you can serve your family?

# FINDING YOUR WAY

*Before I suffered I went the wrong way,*
*but now I obey Your Word.*
PSALM 119:67

The Bible is like a roadmap. It tells how to find your ultimate destination—God. But if you don't read your Bible, you'll just get lost in the chaos of the world.

When you find yourself in tough times, open your Bible. If it says you've done something wrong, you will feel guilt. That's not a bad thing—let God use that guilt to guide you back onto His path.

That's what the psalm writer did. He said that he was going the wrong way, but God's Word showed him where he went wrong. He suffered (that's guilt!). But when he chose to obey God's Word, life was good again. In fact, just a few verses later, he said that God's Word was "better to me than thousands of gold and silver pieces" (verse 72).

Don't be afraid of suffering and guilt. They have a way of leading us back to God.

Thank You, God, for loving me. Help me to stay connected
to You. When I wander, lead me back to You.

Sketch out a map that shows your house and neighborhood.

## THINK ABOUT IT!
In what ways is the Bible like a map?

# PERFECT

*You will keep the man in perfect peace whose mind
is kept on You, because he trusts in You.*
ISAIAH 26:3

Imagine that God is a big, strong bodyguard, working all the time to keep you safe. The Bible says He will fill you with peace as you keep thinking about Him.

Beware of things that will take your mind off God. Sure, movies and video games and sporting events are fun. But if you spend all your time thinking about them, how will you keep your mind on God? Don't let yourself be distracted by the things of the world. If you want to have peace—if you want to be happy and content no matter what's going on around you—you'll have to keep your mind on God.

Look for His wonderful power in your life as He answers your prayers and provides everything you need. God cares deeply for you, and He wants what's best for your life. Remember to always make Him number one, and everything else will fall into place.

God, please help me trust You in everything. Help me remember that You know better than I do! Thank You for caring about me.

Sketch a picture from your favorite movie.

## THINK ABOUT IT!
What are your biggest distractions in everyday life?
Would it be helpful to set time limits on TV and video games?

# WAITING FOR THE REWARD

*"When you give, do not let your left hand know what your right hand gives. Your giving should be in secret. Then your Father Who sees in secret will reward you."*
MATTHEW 6:3–4

It feels good to do nice things for others. People appreciate your help and think good things about you. They might say that you're a nice guy and tell others what a good person you are. There's nothing wrong with any of that. But none of those things are the best reward for doing good.

Jesus says that when you give to others, you should do it in secret. Don't let anyone know that the good deed was yours. Why? Well, if someone on earth praises you for being kind, you've already gotten your reward. There's nothing more. But if *God* is the only one who saw the good thing you did, then He'll give you a reward later in heaven.

It isn't easy to wait for rewards. But the rewards that God promises are always worth the wait.

Lord, help me to do good things for the right reasons. Remind me today that Your rewards are better than earthly praise.

Draw a picture of a trophy.

## THINK ABOUT IT!
Why would Jesus want you to do good things in secret?

# DECIDE, THEN FOLLOW

*He [Moses] chose to suffer with God's people instead
of having fun doing sinful things for awhile.*
HEBREWS 11:25

There are fun, cool, and popular people we want to be friends with. But sometimes they don't make good choices. If you do what they do, your choices won't be the choices God wants you to make.

In the Bible, Moses was adopted into the home of Egypt's king. But first, he'd been born into God's family. When Moses grew up, he chose not to be known as a prince of Egypt, but as someone who followed God.

You might be known as a boy who's good at baseball or lives in a nice house. You could be known as a boy who doesn't play sports at all or never talks about where he lives. None of that is as important as following God.

Sinful things—bad choices—can be fun. For a while. But the Bible says the end of them is death (Proverbs 14:12). Follow Moses' example: decide how you're going to live. Then follow the Lord.

Father, help me choose You instead of the people
who do not follow You. I don't want to get lost.

Sketch some items that tell something about who you are.

## THINK ABOUT IT!
What words do you think others would use to describe you?
How would you describe yourself to someone else?

# TINY TO GOD

*What the Lord had told His servant Moses to do, he told Joshua,*
*and Joshua did it. He did everything the Lord had told Moses.*
JOSHUA 11:15

Many, many years ago there was a brave young man named Joshua. God used him to do great things.

Why? Because Joshua knew how to obey God.

The Lord told Joshua to find new land for the Israelites. Many people were afraid, but Joshua had faith. He led the Israelites to a city named Jericho, which they marched around seven times. Then they blew trumpets and shouted—and watched the giant walls fall, just like God had said they would. Joshua and the people quickly took over the land.

Are there any giant walls in your life? Maybe it's a class at school or some job you don't feel confident doing. Maybe it's a person who doesn't treat you well. Just do what God says and see how He takes care of your problem. What's big to you is tiny to God.

Lord, I want to be brave like Joshua. Sometimes I feel nervous that I'm not strong enough. Thank You for reminding me that my problems are tiny to You.

Draw a picture of the crumbling wall of Jericho.

## THINK ABOUT IT!
Are there any problems that are like giant walls in your life?
Have you asked God to help you deal with them?

# NOT WHAT YOU EXPECTED?

*Naaman was very angry and went away. He said, "I thought he would come out to me, and stand, and call on the name of the Lord his God. I thought he would wave his hand over the place, and heal the bad skin disease."*

2 KINGS 5:11

We humans have a bad habit of wanting to tell God what to do and how to do it. That's kind of like an ant marching up to you and making demands. Crazy, huh?

In the Old Testament, Naaman made that mistake. He had a skin disease called leprosy, and someone told him the prophet Elisha could help. Naaman was from the country of Syria. Elisha sent a messenger to tell him to wash in Israel's Jordan River to be healed.

Naaman, a powerful army commander, couldn't believe it. *Why didn't Elisha himself come out? Why can't I wash in the rivers of Syria instead?*

Happily for Naaman, one of his servants convinced him to do what Elisha said. And Naaman was completely healed.

When God's ways don't make sense, trust Him anyway. He always knows best.

Lord, may I always do what You say,
even when I don't understand.

Sketch a picture of Naaman walking
into the Jordan River to be healed.

## THINK ABOUT IT!
Why should you trust God 100%?

# SET YOUR HOPE

*Set your hope now and forever on the loving-favor to be given you when Jesus Christ comes again.*
1 PETER 1:13

For many kids, childhood is a time of learning, playing, goofing around. . . and not too much stress. But as you get older, you'll realize that life is *not* all fun and games. Really, it can be downright hard. Want proof? Ask your parents or grandparents if they ever struggled to pay bills, worried over a health problem, or wished their kids behaved better.

Part of growing up is dealing with hard things. For most kids, moms or dads or grandparents or teachers protect them from the worst stresses. But the day will come when you're on your own.

Well, not totally on your own. If you're a Christian, you always have Jesus with you. And the Bible says you can "set your hope" on the loving-favor He'll bring when He returns to earth. Whatever hard things you face—now as a kid or later as an adult—will be completely forgotten in Jesus' happy forever.

Lord, thank You for the hope of eternity.
It makes me brave in this life!

Draw a picture of you as a grownup.

## THINK ABOUT IT!
Are you ever really "all on your own"
—even when you're a grownup?

# DO YOU NEED REMINDERS?

*When Abram was ninety-nine years old, the Lord came to him and said, "I am God All-powerful. Obey Me, and be without blame."*
GENESIS 17:1

At home, does your mom or dad ever have to remind you of what you should do? Of course. At practice, does the coach or band director ever need to remind you how to improve your playing? That's why we have coaches and band directors. At school, does your teacher ever have to remind you about your assignments? For most people. . .yep.

Have you ever wondered, *How soon until I don't need reminders all the time?* Well, if Abram (later known as Abraham) is any example, it appears people need reminders as long as they live. He was *ninety-nine* when God said, "Obey Me"!

Like Abraham, we all need reminders of what to do, what is true, and who the Lord is. It's not enough to know these things "once upon a time." We need to keep remembering God's truth each and every day. (That's why it's great that you're reading this book.)

Lord, today I'm glad to be reminded that You are God.
Don't let me forget how to please You!

Sketch a picture of your favorite teacher.

## THINK ABOUT IT!
What qualities make a great teacher or leader?

# FREEZE, FEAR!

*"Do not be afraid. For those who are with us are*
*more than those who are with them."*
2 KINGS 6:16

When your grandfather was your age, the games he played were probably different than the games you play. One game from way back when is called "Capture the Flag." It's an outdoor contest, kind of like freeze tag, in which players try to snatch the flag of the other team without being captured themselves. If you had an extra-large team and could say the words of today's verse—"Those who are with us are more than those who are with them"—you'd be in good shape to win.

Knowing you have help can make you courageous. The prophet Elisha spoke the words above, and he said them because he knew God was with him. God sent help when things were hard. With God's help, Elisha won.

You might feel alone, but God *never* leaves you on your own. And He helps in ways you never thought possible. Because of this, you can freeze fear in its tracks

Lord God, I can't always see the help You send,
but when You do, I love the results.

Draw a picture that represents your favorite game—whether onscreen or outdoors.

## THINK ABOUT IT!
What are some reasons you can "freeze" fear?

# BE ON WATCH

*"Be sure you watch. Pray all the time so that you may be able to keep from going through all these things that will happen and be able to stand before the Son of Man."*

<small>LUKE 21:36</small>

In ancient times, there was a very important job in cities and villages. The watchman stood at a gate or on top of a wall and kept an eye out for threats to the community. That might sound like an easy job, but it took some very strong eyes at nighttime, when all the watchman had was firelight.

God has called us to watch too. We keep an eye out for threats to ourselves and the people we care about. And we pray. We don't have control over the bad things in life, but through prayer, we can talk to the One who *is* in control! We can ask God to watch over our families and friends, our teachers, neighbors and classmates.

Be sure you watch. Pray all the time. Ask God to protect you and your loved ones.

Lord God, help me to be alert to the dangers of this world. Protect me and my family and friends, I pray.

# Draw a picture of a watchman from ancient times.

## THINK ABOUT IT!
### Who is in control of your life?

# NEW-DAY JOY

*Crying may last for a night, but joy comes with the new day.*
PSALM 30:5

Imagine you're going to bed when a loud, flashing thunderstorm blows in. The windows rattle from the wind, the lightning bolts are close enough to sizzle, and the thunder rumbles so heavily you can feel it in your chest. The storm just goes on and on until, somehow, you fall asleep.

But when you wake up, everything is calm. The sun is shining, the birds are singing, the storm is history. In fact, the world feels like a fresh, new place. The rain has washed the dirt off the sidewalks, the grass and flowers are brighter, even the people in your neighborhood seem to be happier.

That's a good picture of the Christian life. This world can be a sad, hard place. There are all kinds of "storms," and whether we want to admit it or not, we feel like crying. But God promises good to His children. He'll bring joy with the new day—whether that's actually tomorrow, or the "new day" of eternity. If you're a Christian, you really can't lose!

God, please give me a happy heart in this sad world.

Sketch a picture that shows your favorite kind of weather.

## THINK ABOUT IT!
How does it make you feel to know that
God promises good things for you?

# GOD GOES WITH YOU

*For I know that nothing can keep us from the love of God. Death cannot! Life cannot! Angels cannot! Leaders cannot! Any other power cannot! Hard things now or in the future cannot! The world above or the world below cannot! Any other living thing cannot keep us away from the love of God which is ours through Christ Jesus our Lord.*

ROMANS 8:38–39

Think about all the things you worry about. Got them in mind? Good. Now, which ones are beyond God's power? Spiders? Nope, God can handle anything with eight legs. Darkness? Ha! God can see in the dark. Your family has to move to another town? It's okay—God's going with you.

Nothing you can imagine would ever take you away from God's love. *Nothing.* You can't even run away from God, because He's already there wherever you go.

Whatever makes you afraid is so much smaller than God's love. That love means you don't have to worry about anything. When you're tempted to worry, read today's verse over and over again.

God, when I feel like I'm all alone, please help me to look for You. Your love never leaves me.

Draw a picture of something that causes you to worry.

## THINK ABOUT IT!
What happens when you give your worries to God?

# COUNT YOUR BLESSINGS

*Happy are the people who have all this.*
*Yes, happy are the people whose God is the Lord!*
PSALM 144:15

One of the wonderful things about the book of Psalms is that it's so real. We read about people who had problems, just like we do. But they still found ways to worship God and find their happiness in Him.

In Psalm 144, the writer makes a long list of good things in his life. He reminds himself of God's loving-kindness, His strength, His protection, and His saving power. Then the psalm writer asks for blessing over his children, his storehouses of food, and his livestock. Happy are the people who have all this, he said. Happy are the people whose God is the Lord!

Get a sheet of paper and make your own list of reasons to be happy. It's okay if it looks different than the psalm writer's. Your list might include your parents, your friends, a safe place to sleep at night, your favorite foods. . . Keep going—you'll be amazed at what God does for you.

Lord, when I count my blessings,
I'm happy that You've taken such good care of me.

Sketch something that God has blessed you with.

## THINK ABOUT IT!
How many blessings can you name in three minutes?

# YOUR SAFE PLACE

*Good will come to the man who trusts in the Lord,
and whose hope is in the Lord.*
JEREMIAH 17:7

God wants you always to trust Him. Your enemy, the devil, wants to tempt you into believing the *world* will meet your needs. Don't believe that—it's simply not true.

God is your safe place. He is the One who gave you life, and who offers you eternal life through Jesus. He is the One who provides food, clothing, and shelter—He created those things and hands them down to you through parents and other concerned adults. He is the One who invented love and joy and all good things, and invites you to find hope in Himself. Your trust in Him opens the door to blessing.

When you're tempted to worry whether you have enough, or to envy the things other people have, or even to lie and cheat to get more, remind yourself of Jeremiah 17:7. Trust in the Lord, and good will come. He is your safe place.

Lord Jesus, teach me how to trust You when things get tough.
Help me to face hard times knowing that You always provide.

Draw a picture of a place that makes
you feel safe and comfortable.

## THINK ABOUT IT!
What makes you feel safe. . .and why?

# HONORABLE MEN

*How happy are the sons of a man who is right
with God and walks in honor!*
PROVERBS 20:7

If you have a great dad, thank God. If your dad isn't so great—or not even around—trust God.

When men become fathers, they're supposed to "bring up a child by teaching him the way he should go" (Proverbs 22:6). Some men do a great job at that. Others don't.

We can't say exactly why God puts some boys in good homes and others in not-so-good homes. But we can say this for sure: God knows everything, and He doesn't make mistakes. So whether you're the happy son of "a man who is right with God" or you can only dream of such a thing, you're right where God put you. The big question is this: Will *you* become a man who "walks in honor"?

You can't change anyone but yourself. If your dad is great, follow his example. If your dad disappoints you, decide to become a better man. God, the perfect Father, will gladly help you to do that.

Lord, help me to become a man who is right
with You, someone who walks in honor.

**Draw a picture of a great dad.**

## THINK ABOUT IT!
What qualities make a great dad?

# THE THINGS GOD DOESN'T DO

*"When you pass through the waters, I will be with you. When you pass through the rivers, they will not flow over you. When you walk through the fire, you will not be burned. The fire will not destroy you."*

ISAIAH 43:2

You cannot go anywhere that takes you away from God. No matter where you are, He's there.

When you're in school and a bully is mean, God is there. When you're home and there's more schoolwork than you think you can handle, He's there. When you're in trouble with your mom or dad because of something you've done, He's there.

God doesn't show up only on days with blue skies. He's there on the days when you've messed up *again*. He's there when other people are rude. He's there to help you with your needs.

God will never leave you, or act like you're a stranger, or pretend He doesn't notice you. Other people might, but God doesn't do anything like that.

He's on your side. No fear required.

Lord, I want to have friends, and I'm disappointed when people let me down. Thanks for being my best Friend. Thanks for noticing me.

Sketch a picture that reminds you of your need for God.

## THINK ABOUT IT!
Is there any time or place that God isn't there with you?

# FAITH PROTECTS

*Most important of all, you need a covering of faith in front of you. This is to put out the fire-arrows of the devil.*
EPHESIANS 6:16

In the Garden of Eden, the serpent fooled Adam and Eve by making them question God's Word. "Did God say," the serpent asked, "that you should not eat from any tree in the garden?" (Genesis 3:1)

Eve answered that they could eat from any tree except the one called "the tree of the knowledge of good and evil." If they ate from that tree, she said, they would die. *Not true!* said the serpent. So Eve took a fruit from the forbidden tree and ate it.

Adam and Eve should have shown more faith in the God who gave them the rules than in the serpent who made them question the rules. If they had, sin would have needed a different way to get into our world. Trusting God protects us from harm. When we listen to people who say something other than what God said, we put ourselves in danger.

Who are you going to listen to today?

Lord, keep me safe from the devil's attacks.
Help me trust You more than anyone else.

Sketch a picture of what you imagine
the Garden of Eden looked like.

## THINK ABOUT IT!
What protects you from making bad decisions
and keeps you from harm?

# MAKE A DIFFERENCE

*Love each other as Christian brothers.*
*Show respect for each other.*
ROMANS 12:10

Christians should be known for their choice to love each other. People should recognize you as a follower of Jesus because you care about others, treat people with respect, and help out when help is needed.

That's a pretty good picture of how Jesus wants you to follow Him. Those are all things that He does, every day, for you.

Have you ever wondered why love is such a big deal to God? Think about it: when you don't show love, you start wanting what other people have, you show disrespect, you wear a frown more often than a smile. Do you like hanging out with people like that? Most people don't.

God is working to make a difference in this world, so He asks *you* to be different too. It's a good difference, one that makes others want to know why you don't act like everyone else.

God, I want to do what others don't because You've asked
me to. I want to obey You by loving my Christian family.
Maybe others will notice and want to know You too.

Sketch a picture of the world.

## THINK ABOUT IT!
What kinds of things can you do to make a difference in your neighborhood, your community, and even the world?

# SHINE BRIGHT

*This is the reason we do not give up. Our human body is wearing out. But our spirits are getting stronger every day.*
2 CORINTHIANS 4:16

Never forget that God thinks you're special. You are a light for Him in a dark world where people have lost their way. Even though you'll have hard times yourself, don't let the struggles put out your flame.

Many people need to hear from you about Jesus. There are other believers who will look to you for encouragement. God will give you strength to serve both Christians and yet-to-be Christians. That's why the apostle Paul told us not to give up—he wanted as many people as possible to know God and to give Him thanks.

When troubles come and you feel tired and weak, ask God to keep you shining bright. Keep praying, keep studying His Word, and God will make your spirit stronger every day.

Lord God, please give me the desire to read my Bible—
and really study it. Help me to know You and be a
light in my world. I want to lead people to Jesus.

Sketch a picture of a lantern.

## THINK ABOUT IT!
How is being a good example in your faith
like shining a bright light for others?

# SEE A NEED? FILL A NEED

*After we were safe on the island, we knew that it was Malta.
The people on the island were very kind to us. It was raining
and cold. They made a fire so we could get warm.*

ACTS 28:1-2

Here's a simple formula for kindness: See a need? Fill a need.

When the apostle Paul got shipwrecked on the island of Malta, the local people treated him with kindness. They saw he was cold and wet, so they made a fire to warm him up. They gave him a place to stay over the winter. When he was ready to leave, they gave him supplies for his journey. The people saw Paul's needs and filled them.

And Paul took care of the people on Malta. With God's help, he healed the island's sick people, loving them in a very practical way.

Look around today and see what needs you can fill. It doesn't have to be a big thing to be a big blessing to someone.

Lord, may I be a blessing today. Help me to see the needs around me and fill them. I pray You would be honored by my actions.

Draw a picture of the people of Malta showing
kindness to Paul after his shipwreck.

## THINK ABOUT IT!
What needs—big or small—can you fill for someone today?

# GREAT THINGS HAPPEN WHEN YOU OBEY

*The one who keeps looking into God's perfect Law and*
*does not forget it will do what it says and be happy*
*as he does it. God's Word makes men free.*

JAMES 1:25

Daniel is a person in the Bible who bravely obeyed God.

He and his friends had been taken far from their own country to serve a distant nation. Because Daniel was wise and hardworking, the kings he worked for trusted him.

But other people were jealous of Daniel, and they tried to get him in trouble. They even tricked the king into throwing Daniel into a pit filled with lions! That must have been scary, but God protected Daniel. When the king got up the next morning, he was amazed to find Daniel still alive.

Daniel told the king that God had sent an angel to shut the mouths of the lions. The king knew that God had helped Daniel, so he made a rule that everyone in his kingdom should worship Daniel's God!

Great things happen when you obey.

Thank You, God, for Daniel. His story gives me courage
to be brave and obey You even when times are tough!

Sketch a picture from the story of Daniel and the lions' den.

## THINK ABOUT IT!
Think about a time when you obeyed God even when it wasn't the easy thing to do. What happened?

# CHEATERS NEVER WIN

*The honor of good people will lead them, but those who hurt others will be destroyed by their own false ways.*
PROVERBS 11:3

There's an old saying that goes, "Winners never cheat, and cheaters never win." But that doesn't always seem true. Sometimes the cheaters *do* win.

Well, cheaters might win for a while, at least. A golfer can secretly nudge his ball into a better spot. A slick-talking salesman might sell someone a bad car. A weak student might steal answers from a straight-A kid's test. It seems like people get away with cheating all the time.

If you find that frustrating, don't forget that God sees everything. He knows who's honest and who's dishonest, who cheats and who lives with honor. And, in the end, God will make everything right. People who refuse to follow Him and His laws will be punished—they'll "be destroyed by their own false ways." But if you follow Jesus and live to obey Him, there will be rewards.

In the long run, the saying *is* true: cheaters never win.

Lord God, help me to live with honor—and to pray for those who cheat. You want them to know You too!

144

# Draw a picture of a game someone might try to cheat at.

## THINK ABOUT IT!
Why do "cheaters never win"?

# MORE IMPORTANT

*"Are not two small birds sold for a very small piece of money?
And yet not one of the birds falls to the earth without your Father
knowing it. God knows how many hairs you have on your head.
So do not be afraid. You are more important than many small birds."*
MATTHEW 10:29–31

Some people don't think they're worth much. They don't seem to have friends, or get along with others, or do very well in school. It's easy to think less of people like that. *Don't.* God never has. And if you think that way about *yourself*, don't. God never has.

He takes care of little birds. He knows how many hairs grow on your head. Does it seem strange for God to keep track of such things? He does, and here's good news: His Word says "you are more important" than them.

If you don't seem to have friends, you have God. If you don't get along with others, He can help. If you don't do very well in school, He can teach.

Don't be afraid. You are important to God.

Father, thank You for seeing me as important. It means a lot.

Sketch a picture of something tiny that God cares about.

## THINK ABOUT IT!
Why does God care about tiny things?

# MAKING PEACE

*My true helper, I ask you to help these women who have worked*
*with me so much in preaching the Good News to others.*
PHILIPPIANS 4:3

There are many ways to help people. You can rake an older man's leaves, carry a single mom's groceries, or set up a fundraiser for a Christian afterschool program. But some people need help of a different kind.

In Philippians 4, the apostle Paul mentioned two women who were arguing. We don't know what the problem was, but Paul said they needed to "agree as Christians should" (verse 2). And Paul asked a man in their church to step in and help them.

This kind of help is called "peacemaking." Sometimes two people in conflict need a third person to walk them through their problems. The third person needs to be gentle, wise, and kind—they need to know what God's Word says and how to live it out.

Maybe someday, that "third person" will be *you*. It takes bravery to help people in conflict, but God gives courage when we ask. And He loves it when we help others to make peace.

Lord, give me courage to help others make peace.

Draw a picture of yourself doing something peaceful.

## THINK ABOUT IT!

Why is it important to be gentle, wise, and kind when you're trying to make peace with another person?

# KEEP LOVING JESUS!

*"Let the little children come to Me.*
*Do not try to stop them."*

LUKE 18:16

Why do boys and girls love Jesus? In the Gospels, it's clear that they loved Jesus because He loved them first. Jesus wasn't posing for artists when He invited kids to gather around. He didn't have to do any coaxing—children loved Him. So did their parents, who were eager for Jesus to bless their kids.

Like a beloved uncle or grandfather, Jesus put His hands on the kids' heads and prayed for them. You can just imagine parents reminding their children, "Do you remember when Jesus prayed for you?" What a wonderful memory that would be.

Some people say that adults who love children are really just kids themselves, at heart. That is, they're people who've held on to the best qualities of childhood. . .including loving Jesus.

So loving Jesus isn't just for boys. It's for young men, middle-aged men, and old men, as well. You could say that loving Jesus is the most important thing you can do in your whole life.

Lord God, I want to keep loving Jesus!

Draw a picture of Jesus spending time with children.

## THINK ABOUT IT!
Why do you think little children loved being around Jesus?

# CHOOSING LAST PLACE

*"Whoever wants to be first among you, must be the
one who is owned and cares for all."*
MARK 10:44

Right before guys play basketball at recess, the two captains start picking players for their teams. Everyone gulps. Okay, maybe not everyone—but some guys are secretly thinking, *I hope I'm not picked last.* That's never fun, is it?

Actually, it can be.

Look again at today's Bible verse. Jesus is talking to His closest friends, and He basically says, "Quit worrying about who I'm going to pick to be captains. Instead, you should be willing to be sat on the bench. Be willing to fetch towels when the other guys come off the court. Serve them and you'll be the *real* captain on My team."

The weird thing? It works. Even though you're doing the grunt work, you really do feel like the top dog.

Every time you line up to play ball or divide into teams for a school project, remember what Jesus said. Serve the other guys (or girls) on your team. Then imagine Jesus watching and cheering for you!

Lord, I believe You. I'm going to choose to serve other people.

Draw a picture showing what it means
to let someone else go first.

# THINK ABOUT IT!
Has someone ever let you go first? How did it make you feel?

# LIKE A TREE ON A RIVERBANK

*Happy is the man who does not walk in the way sinful men tell him
to, or stand in the path of sinners, or sit with those who laugh
at the truth. But he finds joy in the Law of the Lord
and thinks about His Law day and night.*

PSALM 1:1–2

Some things in the Bible are very plain—like the formula for happiness in Psalm 1:1-2.

There are three things to avoid, and one to pursue. The "stay aways" first: Don't befriend people who always make bad choices. Don't walk where they're going, don't stop to hang out with them, and definitely don't sit down to stay. Don't hang out with people who "laugh at the truth"—that is, God and His Word—because they're trouble. They won't bring you happiness.

What will? Well, God and His Word. Make your quiet time a top priority. Read your Bible and pray. When you take the time to listen to what God's saying, then think about it "day and night," you'll be happy. You'll be like a strong, healthy tree on a riverbank (Psalm 1:3).

Lord, may I choose my friends wisely—
and always spend time with You.

Sketch a picture of a tree on a riverbank.

## THINK ABOUT IT!

How does obeying God and focusing on His Word
make you "like a strong, healthy tree on a riverbank"?

# MIRACLES FOR YOUR FAMILY

*He has remembered His agreement forever, the promise*
*He made to last through a thousand families-to-come.*

PSALM 105:8

How good that you have access to God's Word, the Bible. It's even better when you believe God's promises, obey His commands, and enjoy His rich blessings. Those blessings include miracles—incredible things God does for His beloved children.

Over the years, how many miracles has God done for you and your family? If you're not sure, make a list. Ask your dad or mom to help you recognize miracles that God has done for you. Maybe call your grandparents for help. Try to come up with at least four miracles your family has received from God.

Here are some examples: Has God saved anyone's life? Has He healed someone? Has He provided money right when your family needed it? Did He provide just the right house at the right time?

Of course, there are many other kinds of miracles too. Figure out what they are, and then say, "Thanks, God!"

Lord, You do millions of miracles, every day, all around
the world. Help me to recognize the miracles
You have done for me and my family.

Draw a picture that represents a miracle God
has provided for your family.

## THINK ABOUT IT!
How many incredible things has God done for you
and your family through the years?

# GOD WORKS THROUGH US

*O Lord, You will give us peace,*
*for You have done all our works for us.*
ISAIAH 26:12

Some things in life are hard to understand. But that doesn't mean they're not true.

Here's a mystery for you: when you do good things, it's really *God* doing them. He's the one who gives you the desire and ability to say "no" to bad things and "yes" to His own plans. That's what Isaiah was saying in today's verse. It's what the apostle Paul meant when he wrote, "He is working in you. God is helping you obey Him. God is doing what He wants done in you" (Philippians 2:13).

When you dream of doing great things, that's really God's dream. Not a dream to make a million dollars—that's nothing to the God who made (and owns) the whole universe. But dreams of helping people, encouraging people, pointing people to God through His Son, Jesus Christ. . .now those are the dreams that excite God. And when He passes the dream on to you, you'll be exited too!

Let God live His dreams through you.

Lord, please use me to accomplish Your plans in this world.

Sketch a picture showing you doing a great thing—something that's God's dream for you.

## THINK ABOUT IT!
Have you given God control of your life—so you are able to do amazing things for (and through) Him?

# DON'T IGNORE YOUR GIFTS

*We all have different gifts that God has given to us by His loving-favor. We are to use them.*

ROMANS 12:6

What would you love to get next Christmas? A new video game system? A dirt bike? Tickets to a huge sporting event?

Imagine that on Christmas morning, you found the one thing you wanted, tagged with your name. Cool! Then you walked away and never used it.

What? Get a great gift only to ignore it? Never to enjoy it yourself or allow the gift-giver to see you using it? That's crazy.

When you become a Christian, God gives you "spiritual gifts," special abilities you can use to bless others. They include teaching, giving, leadership, and "discernment"— helping people to understand the right things. But you've got to *use* your gift to please God and help others.

Sure, you're still young. But if you sense that God has given you a certain gift, look for ways to use it. Talk to your parents or your pastor and see if there's a place for you to serve. Don't ignore your gifts!

Father God, show me my gifts—then help me use them to please You and help others.

Sketch a scene of what Christmas
morning looks like at your house.

## THINK ABOUT IT!

Is it possible that you've been ignoring the gifts God has
given you? If so, how can you put them to good use?

# EATING AND DRINKING

*This is what I have seen to be good and right: to eat and to drink and be happy in all the work one does under the sun during the few years of his life which God has given him. For this is his reward.*
ECCLESIASTES 5:18

The Bible talks a lot about eating and drinking. And why not? God created food and drinks for us to enjoy. He also put us into families, where we can learn and grow as we're protected from the world around us. When food and family come together, the message of Ecclesiastes 5:18 is true: it's "good and right," a happy reward from God.

But if you're like a lot of boys, you might prefer to do other things than sit down to a family meal. Hey, there are bikes to ride, hoops to shoot, and videos to watch, right? Who wants to hit the brakes for a half hour around the dinner table?

Don't rush through your family dinner. If you do, you're missing one of God's intended gifts. Take your time over food and drink with your family. It's good and right—a reward, even!

Lord, may I enjoy my family mealtime.

Draw a picture of your family enjoying mealtime together.

## THINK ABOUT IT!
What are some good conversation starters you could use to make family dinner more interesting and fun?

# BREAKING THE RULES

*Then the daughter of Pharaoh came to wash herself in the Nile.
Her young women walked beside the Nile. She saw the basket in the
tall grass and sent the woman who served her to get it. She opened it
and saw the child. The boy was crying. She had pity on him
and said, "This is one of the Hebrews' children."*

EXODUS 2:5-6

While they were in Egypt, the people of Israel grew in number. And that made the Egyptians nervous. Finally, Pharaoh decided the Israelites should never get powerful enough to rebel against him. So he ordered that all their male babies should be killed.

Moses' mom disobeyed the order, keeping her baby alive by putting him in a floating basket in the river. Pharaoh's daughter disobeyed the order and adopted Moses as her son. Both women knew that murdering babies was wrong.

God used these rule-breaking women to free the Israelites from slavery. If you ever find human rules that go against God's teaching, you can break them. God will bless you for following Him.

Lord, please give me the wisdom and boldness
to follow Your rules instead of man's.

# Draw a picture of baby Moses.

## THINK ABOUT IT!
When is it okay to be a rule-breaker?

# DON'T BE MAD

*Then [Joseph] sent his brothers away. As they left he said to them,*
*"Do not be mad at each other on the way."*
GENESIS 45:24

If you want to know what forgiveness looks like, this is a great example.

Joseph had been sold into slavery by his brothers. But over many years, God worked a miracle: Joseph became a ruler in his new home of Egypt.

Then came a famine. There was no rain. Crops didn't grow. People began to starve. But God had made Joseph very wise, and he was prepared. Joseph had saved back enough food to save many lives.

His brothers came to Egypt, hoping to buy food. They had to meet with Joseph, but they had no idea this was the brother they had treated so badly.

Joseph, though, recognized his brothers—and *he forgave them.* Then he said something they probably never expected: "Do not be mad at each other." Joseph's brothers expected anger, but Joseph was kind.

Life is always better when you choose to forgive.

God, please help me choose to be kind, to forgive, to love.
Give me courage to choose Your way, even when it's hard.

Draw a picture of the food Joseph saved.

## THINK ABOUT IT!
Read Joseph's story again.
How did Joseph's actions show he was wise?

# CHANGE OF PLANS

*Joseph awoke from his sleep. He did what the angel
of the Lord told him to do. He took Mary as his wife.*
MATTHEW 1:24

There's a story in the Bible about a man who decided to break a commitment. Then God got hold of him and changed his mind. He did what he was originally planning to do—and he was blessed.

The man was Joseph, and his commitment was to become the husband of Mary. That's the Mary who was pregnant with Jesus—but because Joseph knew he wasn't the father, he thought he should walk away from the marriage.

God, though, sent an angel to tell Joseph to do what he'd promised. Mary was pregnant through a miracle, and God wanted Joseph to be her husband. . .and help to raise her boy, who was actually the Son of God!

Joseph obeyed. He trusted that God would work everything out. And two thousand years later, we remember him as the husband of Mary and the "father" of Jesus.

Today, what might God be telling *you* to do?

Lord, please show me what You want me
to do and give me the strength to do it.

Sketch a picture of Mary, Joseph, and baby Jesus.

## THINK ABOUT IT!
How would you react if an angel came to
share a message from God with you?

# PLANT AND HARVEST

*Remember, the man who plants only a few seeds will not have much grain to gather. The man who plants many seeds will have much grain to gather.*
2 CORINTHIANS 9:6

Have you ever noticed how the Bible uses picture-stories to explain ideas? The apostle Paul, who wrote this verse, compares the giving of money to planting seeds. When you plant a few seeds, you only get a small crop. But if you plant a lot of seeds, you get a huge crop.

So when it comes to giving money, Paul says, "Plant a lot!" Give away a lot of money so God can use it in big ways. He'll take what you give and turn it into a big crop—a lot of help to people who need it.

*But what about me?* you might be thinking. *If I give away my money, won't I have needs too?* Yep. And God's got that covered. Just a few verses later, Paul said, "God can give you all you need. He will give you more than enough" (2 Corinthians 9:8).

Lord, I want to be a Christian who is known for loving and helping my fellow Christians.

Sketch a picture that shows what
happens after you plant a seed.

## THINK ABOUT IT!
Why do you think God used picture-stories in the Bible?

# TEAM CHRISTIAN

*I ask you to keep using the gift God gave you. It came to you when
I laid my hands on you and prayed that God would use you.*
2 TIMOTHY 1:6

If you're on a football or robotics or quiz team, you know how important teamwork is. That's true on "Team Christian" too.

Second Timothy is a letter from a wise, older pastor to a younger man learning the ministry. The apostle Paul gave Timothy advice for leading a church, but also urged him to be brave and strong. And Timothy could because he had God's gift of leadership. Paul had confirmed that by laying his hands on Timothy's head and praying that God would use him.

Sometimes we think we need to do everything ourselves. We're afraid to ask for advice or help. Don't be like that! God has put older, wiser men in your life to help you grow. Learn from them, follow their example, and ask for their prayers.

And someday, before you know it, *you'll* be the older, wiser man. You'll become the coach who keeps Team Christian winning.

Lord, please put wise, older men in my life—
and help me to learn from them.

Draw a picture of someone who's given you great advice.

## THINK ABOUT IT!
Name all the people God has placed in your life—
to be teachers, leaders, and advice-givers.

# IF, THEN

*Dear friends, if God loved us that much,*
*then we should love each other.*

1 JOHN 4:11

Have you noticed how the words *if* and *then* go together? *If* you eat too much candy, *then* you'll get a stomachache. *If* you pull a dog's ears, *then* you'll probably get bitten. Those are examples of *if-then* consequences.

But today's verse shows if and then in a different way. *If* God loves us (and He does), *then* we should love each other. You could say, *Because* God loves us, *then* we should share that love with the people around us.

Some people are easy to love. We smile at them, and they smile back. We offer a hand, and they say, "thank you." But others are harder to love. In fact, some people can be downright mean.

But God loved us while we were still sinners (Romans 5:8), so we should show love to anyone and everyone we meet. It may take some bravery on our parts, but God is happy to help. *If* we pray and ask for courage, *then* He will provide it!

Lord God, I want to follow Your example and share Your love.

Sketch out a scene showing an "if, then" consequence.

## THINK ABOUT IT!
How might you use "if, then" scenarios to follow
God's Word and shine your light for others to see?

# REMEMBER GOD, ALWAYS

*On my bed I remember You.*
*I think of You through the hours of the night.*
PSALM 63:6

Your life is really all about God. He made you, and He thinks you're very special. (Reread that last sentence a hundred times if you need to—let its truth sink deep into your mind and heart.) When you understand how important you are to God, you will naturally draw close to Him.

When you feel tired and weak, God is there. He will comfort you in hard times and give you a thousand things to be grateful for. Develop a happy heart by looking around for signs of God's greatness—sunrises and sunsets, mountains and meadows, horses and hawks, friends and family. God's handiwork (and evidence of His love) is all around you.

He loves you with a love that the Bible says is better than anything. So when you go to bed tonight, think about God. He'll be watching over you as you sleep, and He'll lead you into a brave new day tomorrow.

Lord, I thank You for loving me. Even when life is tiring and stressful, I can feel brave knowing that You are in control.

Draw a picture of something that always reminds you of God's love.

## THINK ABOUT IT!
Think about all the things that give you a happy heart. How many can you name?

# ASKING BOLDLY

*"O my God, turn Your ear and hear! Open Your eyes and see our trouble and the city that is called by Your name. We are not asking this of You because we are right or good, but because of Your great loving-pity."*

Daniel 9:18

Daniel was an impressive young guy, maybe only a few years older than you. His country—the Jewish nation of Judah—was attacked and defeated by the army of Babylon. The king of Babylon then rounded up guys like Daniel and took them away to serve in his country. That's where Daniel eventually got in trouble for praying to God. You probably know that he ended up in a den of hungry lions.

Well, God protected Daniel and he came out of the lion's den alive. And he kept praying. One time, he admitted to God that he and his people had really messed up. Their disobedience had led to the ruin of their nation!

But Daniel could boldly ask God for forgiveness. Why? Reread today's verse and pay special attention to the last sentence.

Lord God, I want to be brave in prayer,
not because I'm good, but because You are.

Sketch of picture of Daniel praying to God.

## THINK ABOUT IT!
Why can we ask God for His forgiveness?
(Hint: Reread Daniel 9:18.)

# DON'T FREAK OUT

*"Peace I leave with you. My peace I give to you. I do not give peace to you as the world gives. Do not let your hearts be troubled or afraid."*
JOHN 14:27

What do you think *peace* means? You might believe peace is getting along with your friends and never arguing. You might think it's when one nation decides it won't fight another country.

Peace is actually God's gift to you. Jesus left it for you and with you.

Peace is more than just not fighting. God's peace makes you calm even when hard things come into your life. You can be peaceful (as well as joyful, hopeful, and without worry) no matter what's going on around you. You can stay cool because the God of peace will help you.

Believe in God, and there's nothing to fear. Don't give your heart permission to freak out. God has the perfect answer for your bad days: peace.

Father, I'm most strong when You help me. You take care of my needs, and You tell me I don't have to be troubled or afraid. This isn't easy for me to accept, so please help me.

When you experience something hard,
what brings you peace? Sketch it here.

## THINK ABOUT IT!
Peace is more than just getting along with others.
How many other kinds of "peace" can you think of?

# SAFE AND SOUND

*I am suffering. But I am not ashamed. I know the One in Whom I have put my trust. I am sure He is able to keep safe that which I have trusted to Him until the day He comes again.*

2 TIMOTHY 1:12

What if your neighbor had to go away for a while and asked you to take care of her dog? That's an important responsibility. You would work hard to make sure the dog was fed and watered, exercised and protected. If that dog's life was entrusted to you, you'd make sure it was safe and sound when your neighbor returned home.

That's how the apostle Paul said God handles your life. In a letter to his friend Timothy, Paul said his own life was hard. He was suffering because so many people hurt him. They arrested him, beat him, and threw him in jail for preaching about Jesus. But he knew that God would protect his soul and spirit. Paul had entrusted himself to God, and God would bring Paul safe and sound into heaven.

He will do the same thing for you.

Father, I put my full trust in You. Keep me safe and sound!

# Draw a picture that shows you being responsible.

## THINK ABOUT IT!
In what ways does God keep you safe and protected?

# BE A TEACHER

*In all things show them how to live by
your life and by right teaching.*
Titus 2:7

How old do you have to be to teach? If you want to be a schoolteacher, you'd probably be at least twenty-one. But you can actually start teaching right now.

*Um, me? No way!* Yes, really. *But I don't know how to teach!* Sure you do. *How?* By telling other people what you know. *But I don't know anything!* Of course you do. Just tell what you know is true.

Sometimes you don't even have to do the talking. You could hand this book to a friend and say, "Hey, read page 80. . .then tell me what you think." Then wait quietly. Give him a few minutes to consider the words. Keep waiting quietly until he tells you what he thinks. And then still wait quietly. See what he says when he talks a second time. Answer any questions he might have—and if you need to, ask a parent or your pastor for help with any tough questions.

Yes, it's that easy!

Lord, You made sure I read this book.
Help me to share its message today.

What are you really good at?
Draw a picture of you teaching that skill to someone else.

## THINK ABOUT IT!
What valuable knowledge or skills do you have
that would be worth teaching to others?

# GOOD SAM

*"Then a man from the country of Samaria came by. He went up to the man. As he saw him, he had loving-pity on him. He got down and put oil and wine on the places where he was hurt and put cloth around them. Then the man from Samaria put this man on his own donkey. He took him to a place where people stay for the night and cared for him."*

<small>LUKE 10:33-34</small>

Most everyone has heard of the Good Samaritan. They know that "Good Samaritans" go out of their way to help others.

The story of the Good Samaritan is a parable—a teaching tool—of Jesus. He told about a Jewish man who'd been attacked by robbers and left for dead. Two other Jewish men, both religious leaders, saw the injured man on the roadside but never stopped to help. Who did? A man from Samaria, a place the Jews hated. The Samaritans weren't fond of the Jews either, but this guy did something brave—he helped, and in a big way.

How did Jesus end His story? By saying, "Go and do the same."

**Lord Jesus, show me how to be a "Good Sam"!**

Sketch a picture from the story of the Good Samaritan.

## THINK ABOUT IT!
Why is it sometimes hard to help people who aren't like us?
What does God's Word say about helping others?

# BE SURE OF GOD

*Even if an army gathers against me, my heart will not be afraid.
Even if war rises against me, I will be sure of You.*

PSALM 27:3

Here's a hard thought: we trust a lot of things in this world, but none of them are absolutely certain. Sometimes the brakes fail on the car. Our homes might get knocked down by a hurricane, tornado, or earthquake. Even the people we rely on most can get sick and die.

We can't be sure of anything. . .except God.

But if we have God, we have everything we need! The writer of this verse, David, knew to trust God in the worst times—even if an army rose up in battle against him. David saw God's power in his life many times. (Remember that knockout of Goliath?) And he trusted that God would show that power again.

God doesn't always take His children out of sticky situations. But He has promised that He will never leave us or give us up (Hebrews 13:5). What do you have to fear when you can be sure of God?

Lord, You are always faithful. Help me to be confident in You.

Draw a picture of something or someone you trust.

## THINK ABOUT IT!
What are some reasons you can trust God 100%?

# LOVE = OBEDIENCE

*Jesus said, "The one who loves Me will obey My teaching.*
*My Father will love him. We will come to him and live with him."*
JOHN 14:23

A man named John the Baptist spent his life telling people about Jesus. He didn't travel the world and put on big shows. He lived a simple life—out in the desert, wearing clothes made of camel hair, eating wild honey and locusts (bugs like grasshoppers). Can you imagine?

One day, Jesus came to John, asking to be baptized. John didn't feel like he was good enough to baptize Jesus, but Jesus said that was just the way it should be.

So John obeyed—and then he kept telling people about Jesus. He didn't worry what others thought of him. He didn't waste time wondering how he could become popular. Because John was more interested in Jesus than in himself, God used him to accomplish great things.

And God can use you in the same way. If you love Jesus, obey His teaching. Be like John the Baptist and tell the world about your Lord.

Dear Jesus, please help me to obey Your plan for my life.

Draw a picture of John the Baptist
(read a description of him on page 190).

## THINK ABOUT IT!
When it comes to obeying God, should you care
what other kids might think? Why or why not?

# GRAB YOUR SWORD!

*God's Word is living and powerful. It is sharper than a sword that cuts both ways. It cuts straight into where the soul and spirit meet and it divides them. It cuts into the joints and bones. It tells what the heart is thinking about and what it wants to do.*

HEBREWS 4:12

A writer named J. R. R. Tolkien created a fantasy world called Middle Earth. It was filled with creatures like hobbits, elves, dwarves, and talking trees. Two of his hobbit characters, Bilbo and Frodo Baggins, used a special sword named Sting. It would glow blue whenever the ugly, evil orcs were nearby.

In some ways, the Bible is like Sting. It calls itself a sword, and we can use it to defend ourselves from the devil's attacks. And the Bible also warns us of coming trouble. It gets deep into our own thoughts and desires to tell us when we're on the wrong path.

But even better, the Bible shows us the *right* way to go. We can always be bold when we're doing what God's Word says.

Lord, I am protected by Your Word.
Help me to handle this "sword" skillfully!

Draw a picture of your "sword," the Bible.

## THINK ABOUT IT!
What does it mean that "God's Word is living and powerful"?

# NO FEAR IN OBEDIENCE

*Say to those whose heart is afraid, "Have strength of heart,
and do not be afraid. See, your God will come ready to punish.
He will come to make sinners pay for their sins, but He will save you."*
ISAIAH 35:4

Does it seem that different people play by different rules? Your mom or dad tells you to respect others, but no one else seems to do that. You're told to be kind, but many people are rude. You're asked to love others, but some people you know just seem to spread hate.

In the Bible, God gave the rules that He wants people to follow. Some people ignore the rules, and others just refuse to follow them.

Isaiah was one of God's messengers called "prophets." He saw many people making excuses for ignoring God's rules. Isaiah knew that those people would face consequences for their disobedience. Someday, God would make them pay.

But if you want to obey God, Isaiah had good news: you can be strong knowing that you will be saved. There is no fear in obedience.

Father, obeying You means I'm willing to follow
You in the greatest adventures of life.

Sketch a sign in the space below that would
be a good rule for people to follow.

## THINK ABOUT IT!
Why is it important to follow God's rules for living?

# SHADOW OF WINGS

*My soul goes to You to be safe. And I will be safe in the
shadow of Your wings until the trouble has passed.*
PSALM 57:1

God loves you and shows you kindness in so many ways. This truth should
help you trust Him no matter what's happening. God will always lead you
in the right way. Your job is to spend time with Him, reading His Word
and praying and "listening" for what He tells you to do.

Psalm 57 was written by David, who was running for his life from the
jealous King Saul. Even when he was hiding in a cave, David called to
God for help. His enemies were trying to distract him, but David kept his
attention on the Lord.

How can you keep your focus on God? Think about the times of your
day when you worry or wonder. Turn those into Bible reading and prayer
times! Trust God to help you overcome your fears. He promises to keep
you safe, like a baby bird under the protective wings of its mother.

Lord God, I thank You for keeping me safe from the troubles
of this world. May I always keep my focus on You.

Draw a picture of David hiding in a cave.

## THINK ABOUT IT!
How can you keep your focus on God—
and away from the distractions in your life?

# GO AHEAD AND ASK

*Jesus said to him, "What do you want Me to do for you?"*
*The blind man said to Him, "Lord, I want to see!"*
MARK 10:51

"Blind Bart" sat at the roadside, begging for money. Everyone entering or leaving Jericho saw him there, day after day, scraping up money to live on.

One day, when he learned the miracle-working Jesus was nearby, Bart (full name: Bartimaeus) started shouting: "Jesus, Son of David, take pity on me" (Mark 10:48). Jesus heard Bart, stopped, and called him over. Then Jesus asked what he wanted.

"Oh, nothing," Bart answered. "I just thought I'd say hi."

*Um, no.* Blind Bart was quick to answer, "Lord, I want to see!"

If you're a follower of Jesus, God *wants* you to ask for things—your daily food, forgiveness of your sins, protection from temptation. You can also ask for your friends to know Jesus, wisdom in decision-making, even—like Bart—healing for yourself and others.

Sometimes God will say "no" to your requests. . .but until He does, go ahead and ask. He might very well say, "Yes!"

Lord God, I want to see everything You
have for me in Your Word.

Draw a picture from the story of Bartimaeus.

## THINK ABOUT IT!
What are you asking God for today?

# GLAD IN GOD

*May the words of my heart be pleasing to Him.*
*As for me, I will be glad in the Lord.*
PSALM 104:34

Do you ever wonder how big God is? You should—because the bigger He is to you, the more you will enjoy Him. He is the wonderful Creator who made you. He sets the rules and guides you in the way you should go. He is great and glorious, wise and loving.

Everything we see reflects God's mighty design. He takes care of the land and the animals. He guards the trees and guides the rivers. Nothing is an accident! A time may come when you wonder about your purpose in the world. Don't fret—God is always leading and protecting you.

Because of that, you can keep a positive perspective even when life seems crazy. Let your life be a song that you sing to God in thanksgiving. Let your thoughts and actions be the worship you lift up to Him in praise.

Lord God, I want to stay positive. Some days that's hard
to do, so please show me how to be faithful despite
my circumstances. I want to be glad in You!

Draw a picture of a person or thing that makes you glad in the Lord.

## THINK ABOUT IT!
How big is God?

# CAN'T MICROWAVE THIS

*The Lord is good to those who wait for Him,
to the one who looks for Him.*
LAMENTATIONS 3:25

Microwaves are great. You stick a bag of popcorn inside, and get a hot, fresh snack in a couple minutes. A bowl of ravioli could take even less time.

But microwave ovens can make us think *everything* should go fast. And that's not how life works—especially not the Christian life. Many times, God wants us to slow down, to be patient, to wait for Him to move in our lives. If we expect microwave results, we'll be frustrated. We won't please God, and we won't help anyone else.

That's why brave boys live out the message of Lamentations 3:25. They know that God is good to the guys who wait for Him. They know that God blesses boys who patiently watch for Him.

How do we do that? We get to know Him through His Word. We pray as often as we can. Every time we stop to remind ourselves that God is there (and in control), we gain His goodness in our lives.

Lord, life is not a microwave.
Please help me to be patient!

Draw a picture of something slow.

## THINK ABOUT IT!
What are some things that are worth waiting for. . .and why?

# WHO'S DRIVING?

*Jesus said to His followers, "If anyone wants to be My follower,
he must forget about himself. He must take up his cross and follow Me."*
MATTHEW 16:24

Imagine you're a car. Go ahead, pick your favorite. It's probably a nice one, right? So, who will you allow to drive you? After all, you're a sharp, expensive vehicle.

Would you let your twelve-year-old friend drive? How about a stranger? Probably not. You might not trust them to be as careful as they should be. They might drive too fast, hit a guardrail (maybe even a pedestrian), or never bring you back to the garage. Whew, it's dangerous to be a hot car!

Of course, you're *not* a car. But you still have to be careful who drives (you could say "influences") your life. Many people will tell you the wrong things and point you in the wrong direction. But not Jesus.

Do what He says in the Bible, and you'll never go wrong. When Jesus "drives" you, He'll never scratch your paint or dent your fender. He'll steer you straight into the perfection of heaven.

Lord, make me wise enough to know that
I should always follow where You lead.

Draw a picture of your favorite kind of car or truck.

## THINK ABOUT IT!

Who are some of the influencers in your life—good and bad?
Do you need to make any changes in the people
you're choosing to spend time with?

# CALL ON THE LORD TODAY

*"Look for the Lord while He may be found.*
*Call upon Him while He is near."*
ISAIAH 55:6

When you're young, it seems like you have all the time in the world. A whole year—from birthday to birthday or Christmas to Christmas—feels like forever. But if you're twelve or ten or even eight right now, you can remember a lot of years that have already passed. Someday you'll wake up and realize that you're an adult, that life has actually flown by. It happens to everyone.

And that's why we have verses like Isaiah 55:6 above. If life is like fog ("you see it and soon it is gone," James 4:14 says), then *right now* is the time to "look for the Lord." *Right now* is the time to "call upon Him." God is just waiting for you to say, "Yes, Lord—I believe in You, I trust in You, I want Jesus Christ to be my Savior."

Have you made that call yet? God is on the other end, just waiting to answer.

Father in heaven, I want to be part of Your family.
I call on You today for salvation through Jesus Christ.

# Draw a picture of the "today" you.

## THINK ABOUT IT!
Have you trusted God to be your Savior?

# MORE ENCOURAGEMENT AND ADVENTURE FOR BRAVE BOYS LIKE YOU!

## *100 Adventurous Stories for Brave Boys*

Boys are history-makers! And this deeply compelling storybook proves it! This collection of 100 adventurous stories of Christian men—from the Bible, history, and today—will empower you to know and understand how men of great character have made an impact in the world and how much smaller our faith (and the biblical record) would be without them.

Hardback / 978-1-64352-356-9 / $16.99